THE ART OF GOING SLOW

HOW TO SIMPLIFY YOUR LIFE, CALM YOUR MIND, AND FOCUS ON WHAT TRULY MATTERS TO YOU!

DAMON ZAHARIADES

ARTOFPRODUCTIVITY.COM

CONTENTS

PART III
**HOW TO EMBRACE THE ART OF GOING
SLOW ACROSS YOUR LIFE**

OTHER BOOKS BY DAMON ZAHARIADES

~

THINK BIG

How to Lead a Disciplined Life

The Mental Toughness Handbook

The Procrastination Cure

To-Do List Formula

80/20 Your Life!

The Time Chunking Method

How to Make Better Decisions

The Art of Living Well series

The Art Of Saying NO

The Art of Letting GO

The Art of Finding FLOW

The 30-Day Productivity Boost series

The 30-Day Productivity Plan - VOLUME I

The 30-Day Productivity Plan - VOLUME II

Self-Help Books for Busy People series

Small Habits Revolution

The Joy Of Imperfection

The P.R.I.M.E.R. Goal Setting Method

Improve Your Focus and Mental Discipline series

Fast Focus

Morning Makeover

Digital Detox

Visit ArtofProductivity.com for a complete list of titles and summaries. All titles are available for purchase in ebook, paperback, hardcover, and audiobook formats at ArtofProductivity.com/Amazon.

YOUR FREE GIFT

~

I want to give you a gift as a thank you for purchasing this book. It's my 40-page PDF action guide, *Catapult Your Productivity! The Top 10 Habits You Must Develop to Get More Things Done.*

It's short enough to read quickly but meaty enough to offer actionable advice that can make a real difference in your life.

You can get immediate access to *Catapult Your Productivity* by clicking the link below and joining my mailing list:

http://artofproductivity.com/free-gift/

In the following pages, we will do a deep dive into creating a slower-paced lifestyle. We'll discuss the reasons to embrace it, the challenges you'll encounter, and how to overcome them. Much of what we'll cover will seem counterintuitive at first. But if you stick with me, I promise the journey will be worthwhile.

Onward.

NOTABLE QUOTABLES ABOUT
GOING SLOW

Nature does not hurry, yet everything is accomplished.

— LAO TZU

When we rush, we skim the surface and fail to connect with the richness of the present moment.

— CARL HONORÉ

Slow is smooth. Smooth is fast.

— U.S. NAVY SEALS

INTRODUCTION

❧

I was wrong about productivity.

In the 1990s, I became interested in productivity. True to my addictive personality, this curiosity soon turned into an obsession. Everything I did became an exercise in living productively. I tracked my time like a scientist conducting an experiment. I treated *wasted* time like a leaky faucet; it was an irritating problem that needed to be fixed ASAP.

I fixated on getting more done and doing so at any cost. The longer my to-do list, the greater the challenge, and I looked forward to it each day.

But I got it wrong. *Entirely* wrong. And this mistake severely undermined my quality of life. I unwittingly shed personal attributes that were important to me and replaced them with attributes that were improper and even shameful. I went from being welcoming and patient with others to being dismissive and impatient. I went from being contemplative and calm to being impulsive and easily agitated.

Worst of all, I didn't notice these changes as they happened to me. I became aware of them years later after they had established a foothold in my temperament. After the damage had been done.

What was the cumulative result of these unfortunate changes? My relationships were in shambles. My business was on life support. And most disastrously, my headspace was in a tailspin. I was constantly anxious and short-tempered. I lived on a razor's edge emotionally; the slightest inconvenience would cause me to erupt. And moments of contentment and joy were short-lived, forgotten almost as soon as they happened. My long-suffering friends and loved ones walked on eggshells around me.

This was the price of getting productivity wrong.

Hindsight is a humbling mentor. With some prudence and mindfulness, I could have avoided the heartache and stress. With a modicum of self-awareness, I could have avoided the frustration and despair. But I had sacrificed these qualities on the altar of productivity.

I got a lot done in those days. But the price was far too high. And I'm still feeling the effects today, decades later.

This is the reason I wrote *The Art of Going SLOW*. First, I hope to demonstrate how easy it is to fall into the trap of living a busy, frantic lifestyle focused on getting things done.

Second, I want to throw you a lifeline. If you're feeling constantly stressed, under pressure, and burnt out, I want you to know you can change your circumstances. Of course, I'll show you how to slow down, but that's just the beginning. I'll also show you how to truly *embrace* slowness so that your quality of life improves for years to come.

This is more difficult than it sounds because we'll need to unravel a lot of internal programming. Our bad habits run deep. I'll give you the step-by-step process that changed everything for me. I'm confident it will for you, too.

Along the way, you'll discover something fascinating. Shunning the workaholic lifestyle and slowing down can paradoxically — and dramatically — *improve* your productivity.

But I'm getting ahead of myself. We'll get to that later.

That's a promise.

Damon Zahariades
Art of Productivity
October 2024

WHAT YOU'LL LEARN IN THE ART OF GOING SLOW

❧

I f you've looked at the table of contents for this book, you'll have noticed that we're going to cover a lot of material. It might seem intimidating. Rest assured that we're going to move through it quickly. We're not going to waste time with semi-relevant anecdotes.* Nor will we get bogged down by research that offers limited *practical* value concerning your everyday life.†

I want this book to be inspiring, thought-provoking,

---

* It is considered a "best practice" to include dozens of anecdotes when writing a self-improvement book. While a few stories can help demonstrate ideas, including more is primarily a way to increase the book's word count. I believe the best self-improvement books help the reader take purposeful action as quickly as possible. To that end, I won't include needless stories.

† I've found that very few readers care to read research papers. I don't blame them. Many studies are expensive to access, and most are a chore

and enjoyable. So, we'll keep a fast pace. We'll address every topic thoroughly, but we won't dilly-dally.

With that in mind, here's a quick overview of what we're going to cover in *The Art of Going SLOW*:

Part I

It's easy to overlook the many rewards of slowing down. Likewise, it's easy to brush aside the consequences of living in a constant rush. I made this mistake for years. In **Part I**, I'll make the case for embracing a slower lifestyle. We'll explore how living mindfully and intentionally will improve every aspect of your life.

Part II

I'll describe the step-by-step process I used to slow down my life. There are ten core steps, and we'll discuss each in detail. You'll learn how to apply each step in *your* life and why you should. **Part II** is a mini workshop. The priority is application. So, each step is accompanied by a quick exercise designed to help you to take action.

---

to read. Most importantly, the insight they offer is difficult to apply to real life.

Part III

Slowing down might seem to clash with setting and achieving your goals. It might seem to conflict with the notion of getting ahead and making things happen. In **Part III**, we'll investigate how going slow will help you accomplish everything you want while creating a rich and rewarding lifestyle.

How to Get The Most Value From This Book

Everyone reads self-improvement books differently. Some skim. Some focus exclusively on chapters that seem relevant to them at the moment and disregard everything else. Some read every chapter thoroughly and move on to another self-improvement book when they finish.

I suggest using the following approach with *The Art of Going SLOW*:

1. Read each chapter with a small notebook at your side. Jot down notes as they occur to you. Review your notes after you finish a chapter before moving on to the next one. Ask yourself how to apply what you've read to your daily life.
2. After reading each chapter in **Part II**, create a small plan to implement the material. List five simple things you can do effortlessly in your daily routine. I'll give you plenty of ideas in each chapter to prompt your creative juices.

3. Do the exercises in **Part II**. They're quick and easy, and they'll help you adopt the practices outlined in each chapter.

4. After you finish reading the book, practice the small plans you created while reading **Part II**. Life transformation occurs through *application*.

5. Revisit select chapters as a refresher down the road on an as-needed basis.

That's enough preliminary stuff. Let's dig in.

PART I

THE CASE FOR SLOWING DOWN

∽

You live a fast-paced, hectic lifestyle. When you wake up in the morning, you immediately feel the pressure of the day ahead: obligations, commitments, appointments, meetings, and a mile-long to-do list.

With a groan, you drag yourself out of bed. You shower groggily, throw on clothes, wolf down a quick breakfast (or just a cup of coffee), and rush out the door. As you do so, you prepare yourself mentally to fight morning traffic on the way to work.

The pressure doesn't let up when you arrive at your workplace. It builds. Every task is urgent. Every email and phone call demands an instant response. Every project requires your immediate attention. When the workday finally and mercifully ends, you're exhausted. And you still have to fight traffic on your way home.

Does this sound familiar? Does the above reflect your daily routine? Or worse, is this routine so hardcoded into your day-to-day experience that you no longer notice it?

If you answered yes to any of these questions, it's time to make a positive change that will help you to reclaim your life. It's time to let go of the constant pressure you're feeling. It's time to give yourself the freedom to savor the present instead of frantically chasing the future.

It's time to slow down.

IMPROVE YOUR MENTAL HEALTH AND EMOTIONAL BALANCE

> It's not the load that breaks you down; it's the way you carry it.
>
> — LOU HOLTZ

It's shockingly easy to neglect self-care in a perpetual rush. When every task seems urgent and every problem seems like an emergency, they become the priority. Meanwhile, self-care, the benefits of which form gradually, is placed on the back burner. Worse, the constant push to get more done — to always be doing *something*, often just for the sake of being productive — intensifies this feeling of urgency.

It takes a toll. It chips away at your mental and emotional well-being. Over time, it traps you in a continuous state of anxiety and overwhelm. This is the road to exhaustion and burnout. This is the path to despair and depression.

When you intentionally slow down, you give your mind time to recuperate. To rest and recharge. You step away from your day's chaos, clamor, and manufactured (and pointless) pressures. You allow your mind to heal, regain control, and become more resilient.

Reduce Your Stress

Stress is the body's fight-or-flight response. When your brain perceives a threat, it triggers this response to ensure your survival. Cortisol courses through your body; your blood pressure rises; your focus sharpens; your alertness expands. Stress can literally save your life.

But this response and its accompanying effects are supposed to be temporary. Once you're out of danger, your stress level is supposed to plummet, giving your mind and body time to relax.

When you are in a constant rush, you experience *persistent* stress. The stress is always present. While its purpose is less consequential (your survival isn't at stake), it triggers the same physiological responses. Over an extended period, these effects produce numerous cognitive and emotional issues, such as anxiety and depression.

When you ease the pressure to hurry, you alleviate your body's fight-or-flight response. The pace of your lifestyle no longer continuously activates this response's hormonal and physiological effects. You no longer feel as though you're in a constant state of mental distress.

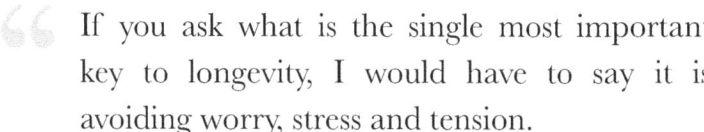
> If you ask what is the single most important key to longevity, I would have to say it is avoiding worry, stress and tension.
>
> — GEORGE BURNS

Manage Your Emotions

Your emotions are powerful. They guide your behaviors and influence your decisions. They sway how you respond to everything that happens to you and can shape your general outlook on life. Your emotions impact the health of your relationships, the trajectory of your career, and your overall sense of satisfaction.

When you live a frantic lifestyle, always striving to do more, the perpetual stress you experience makes it difficult to regulate your emotions. You become less aware of factors that expose you to growing frustration and anger. You become less inclined to guard against impulsiveness and recklessness. You become less vigilant about the potential consequences of bad choices and poor behaviors (e.g., angry outbursts).

Simply put, you lose control.

When you slow the pace of your life, you give yourself

time to tap into your body's soothing system.* This system puts you in a peaceful state and allows you to manage your emotions without feeling threatened. Your soothing system gives you more control and ultimately makes you more resilient.

 Your emotions are the slaves to your thoughts, and you are the slave to your emotions.

— ELIZABETH GILBERT

Improve Your Resilience

Your resilience is your ability to bounce back when you experience a setback or crisis. To clarify, we're not talking about your physical resilience. Instead, we're talking about your mental and emotional resilience.

How do you respond when unfortunate and unpleasant things happen to you? Do you recover quickly and face them with discipline, grace, and courage? Or do you have trouble coping with them or moving forward?

Life in the fast lane counteracts resilience. It prevents its development. This is because resilience grows stronger by practicing mindfulness. When you're always on the go, there's no time to be mindful about life's struggles. There's

---

* This is also known as the parasympathetic nervous system (PSNS). It's a set of neural pathways that helps you relax after a threat is resolved and your body's fight-or-flight response is no longer needed.

no time to confront adverse events to improve how you respond to them.

Slowing down allows you to face challenging situations head-on. It also gives you an opportunity to learn how to navigate adversity down the road. You discover how to overcome obstacles, bouncing back from them rather than feeling overwhelmed.

 Our greatest glory is not in never falling, but in rising every time we fall.

— CONFUCIUS

BOOST YOUR PRODUCTIVITY AND EFFICIENCY

> 66 Slowing down isn't about protesting work. It's instead about finding a better way to do it.
>
> — CAL NEWPORT

We commonly associate productivity with busyness. The busier we are, the more productive we appear. But as you know, this is a mirage. You probably know people who always seem busy but accomplish little. Perhaps you've struggled with this problem yourself in the past. Maybe you struggle with it today.

This error stems from how we frame the relationship between time, effort, and the number of tasks we cross off our to-do lists. We wrongly assume that being productive means always using our spare time. We mistakenly presume that the harder we work and the more effort we expend, the greater our productivity. Meanwhile, crossing items off our to-do lists fuels this delusion. Doing it *feels* productive.

Today's culture has not helped dispel this falsity. Instead, it continues to perpetuate it. Jam-packed schedules are applauded. Hustle is encouraged. Busyness is celebrated. Mile-long to-do lists are revered. Conversely, living life leisurely is often seen as unseemly, even disgraceful.

But here's a paradox of productivity: slowing down can make you *more* productive. Life in the slow lane can lead to greater efficiency, sharper focus, and fewer mistakes.

Achieve More by Doing Less

You've heard the saying, "Work smarter, not harder." It's a cliché, and it sounds vapid in its simplicity. But in fact, it's helpful advice, particularly in the context of increasing your productivity and efficiency. Doing less will likely help you to accomplish more.

Think about every task you spend time and energy on during a typical day. You'll probably have trouble recalling most of them. Some of them you do because you've always done them. Some you do simply because they're on your to-do list. Some you do because you feel obligated to do them.

The reality is that most of these tasks won't help you to achieve your goals. They keep you busy. They make you *feel* productive. But they don't help you to accomplish things that are important to you. This circumstance reflects the 80/20 rule.

The 80/20 rule proposes that 80% of your results spring from 20% of your efforts. To put this another way, 80% of your efforts are wasted. This 80% has a negligible impact on your goals. It affects nominal progress. By abandoning it and focusing your time and energy on the 20% generating the bulk of your results, you "work smarter, not harder."

You do less. Counterintuitively, you achieve more.

> The key to success is not in doing more, but in doing less with absolute focus.
>
> — LEO BABAUTA

Fine-Tune Your Focus

Hustle culture pushes you always to be doing *something* to get closer to your goals. You're encouraged to work longer hours. Network with more people. Negotiate more deals. If you're not hustling, you're not doing enough. If you're not dedicating your time and energy to "making things happen," you're not living up to your potential.

This is toxic productivity. It sounds glamorous. But it leads to stress, disappointment, and exhaustion. And more often than not, it causes burnout.

This lifestyle erodes your ability to focus. When you're

constantly grinding, it isn't easy to concentrate on the tasks that truly matter to you (i.e., the 20%). Your attention is spread thinly across everything you desperately do to "make things happen." Consequently, you lose sight of your priorities. You forget your purpose.

When you slow down, you give yourself the freedom to focus on the things that are important to you. You allow yourself to reflect on your priorities and concerns. You give yourself time to do the deep, creative work that helps you to achieve your goals.

Spending less time and energy on pointless hustling frees you to perform more focused, meaningful work.

> That's been one of my mantras - focus and simplicity... You have to work hard to get your thinking clean to make it simple. But it's worth it in the end because once you get there, you can move mountains.
>
> — STEVE JOBS

Make Fewer Mistakes

Rushing leads to oversights, mishaps, and miscalculations. These errors take time to correct and harm your productivity and efficiency in the long run.

Recall times you hurried to get something done only to make avoidable mistakes that resulted in unnecessary delays. For example, maybe you raced to complete a work-related project only to neglect a critical step. Or perhaps you hurriedly cooked a meal for your family only to inadvertently leave out key ingredients. Or maybe you rushed to write an important email only to allow typos and misspellings to get through.

When you're in rush mode, it *feels* like you're being productive. It *feels* like you're getting things done at a record pace. But there's a good chance you're making mistakes that are causing you to fall behind.

When you work slower, you can work more meticulously. You no longer feel hurried. You no longer feel the constant tug of mild panic and anxiety that you feel when you're in rush mode. This allows you to be more deliberate and cautious. You avoid making mistakes that would otherwise be detrimental to your productivity and efficiency in everything you do.

 Great haste makes great waste.

— BENJAMIN FRANKLIN

STRENGTHEN YOUR RELATIONSHIPS

> The best gift you can give someone is your time, because you're giving them something you'll never get back.

— RICK WARREN

Living a frenetic, always-on-the-go lifestyle has two adverse effects on your relationships. First, it puts unnecessary strain on them. When you constantly do things, you have less energy and attention for your friends and loved ones. So you spend less quality time with them. Meanwhile, your stress levels increase, making you less patient, compassionate, and supportive. Maintaining healthy relationships is hard enough with the added pressure that hustle culture places on them.

The second negative effect is that it's harder to form meaningful relationships. While it's easy to meet people, developing connections with them that extend beyond the surface level is much more difficult. You interact with people, smiling and laughing, but share little intimacy with them. The bonds are weak because life in the fast lane doesn't allow you time to strengthen them.

Living slowly solves these issues. When you slow down, you have more time, attention, and energy to spend on the relationships that are important to you. You form deeper connections. And you have the freedom to nurture them.

Develop Stronger Connections

If you struggle to connect with others, you're not alone. While many factors can contribute to this problem (e.g., lack of confidence, trust issues, personality disorders, etc.), one of the most impactful is a relentlessly busy lifestyle.

The faster you speed through life, the less freedom you have to spend time deepening the level of intimacy you share with people. Conversations remain superficial, and emotional depth remains shallow. Genuine empathy never materializes (when it does, it's fleeting). There's neither time nor energy to invest in developing and nurturing stronger connections.

Committing to a slower pace frees up the time, energy, and attentional resources you need to build strong emotional connections with others. You can enjoy stimulating conversations. You can foster trust, which is necessary to form deeper-seated bonds. You can show genuine kindness, honesty, support, and compassion, which are prerequisites for cultivating empathy.

 The connections we make in the course of a life – maybe that's what heaven is.

— FRED ROGERS

Celebrate Significant Events

The irony of speeding through life is that most people do it to achieve something, yet neglect to celebrate — or even recognize — their achievements. They're so focused on *doing* things that they fail to acknowledge what they've done. They overlook the goals they've accomplished. They ignore the milestones they've reached. They fail to commemorate important events and noteworthy occasions.

There are many reasons to slow down and celebrate life's meaningful moments. Doing so creates fond memories to draw upon when you're feeling emotionally exhausted. It reinforces your sense of purpose and intention. When you celebrate with others, you can nurture the bonds you share with them. Shared celebration cultivates a feeling of community and camaraderie. It fosters trust, compassion, and empathy. It solidifies the rapport that sustains your relationships.

It can be as simple as giving a heartfelt gift to a loved one on their birthday. Or enjoying a weekend excursion with your spouse on your wedding anniversary. Or taking a friend out to dinner to toast a business deal they successfully negotiated.

Celebrating such events is important—even crucial. But it's only possible when you give yourself permission to slow down and invest the time and energy.

> Life is a grand celebration, every moment an opportunity to dance.

— OSHO

Improve Your Communication

Hustle culture has heavily influenced the way we communicate with each other. We used to have honest conversations, discussing thoughts and ideas and learning from one another. We used to take time to listen, reflect, and deliberate.

Today's rise-and-grind ethos and its focus on hyperbusyness changed that entirely. We now communicate with short texts, emails, and tweets. In person, the conversation has been replaced with pithy, snappy exchanges. These are often terse or curt in the pursuit of brevity. The shorter, the better, all in the name of moving forward and doing more — or at least doing *something*. We no longer discuss thoughts and ideas as much as we listen for soundbites that align with our opinions. There's no time to learn, reflect, and deliberate.

This practice has harmed our relationships. It has eroded the rapport we once felt with those around us. It has whittled away the intimacy and kinship we once shared with them. It has replaced the camaraderie we used to enjoy with a relentless drive to *do* more.

When you slow down, you give yourself time to relearn how to communicate in a way that deepens your intimacy with people who are important to you. You also allow yourself to repair atrophied relationships. You can also create and nurture *new* relationships beyond the surface-level interactions that have become the norm in today's always-on-the-go climate.

As your relationships improve, so too does your quality of life. They fuel your happiness, offer comfort during difficult times, and give you a greater sense of purpose.

> The way we communicate with others and ourselves ultimately determines the quality of our lives.

— TONY ROBBINS

ELEVATE YOUR JOY AND SENSE OF FULFILLMENT

"" In today's rush, we all think too much, seek too
much, want too much and forget about the joy
of just being.

— ECKHART TOLLE

There's a sad irony in today's social milieu of
rushing around 24/7. People adopt a rise-and-
grind attitude, putting in long hours and always
seeking to do more because they hope it'll bring them
happiness. This happiness might come in the form of
professional success, financial independence, or a general
sense of accomplishment.

But this lifestyle comes at a steep cost that sabotages
their intention. It prevents them from savoring the

moment, which would bring them happiness *right now*. They sacrifice joy and fulfillment in the present to experience both down the road, a result that isn't guaranteed. Worse, this enormous sacrifice often leads to regret and bitterness, which undermine their future happiness.

It's not entirely their fault. Hustle culture shames leisure and relaxation. It shames living a slower-paced life.

The good news is that you're in control. You can break away from this mindset, a self-defeating attitude fueled by society's wrongheaded productivity doctrine. Once you do so, you'll free yourself to revel in the moment, experiencing joy and fulfillment *now* rather than forfeiting it for a future that might never materialize.

Recognize Your Small Wins

You're used to celebrating big accomplishments. A promotion at work, buying your first house, building a successful business. You worked hard. You invested a lot of time and energy. You achieved a significant goal. You earned it, and you deserve to celebrate.

But do you also acknowledge your smaller wins? Do you take the time to recognize the tiny victories you experience each day? These include finishing a minor project at work, completing your morning routine without distraction, providing emotional support to a friend, or learning something new that you can use immediately.

Recognizing these smaller achievements is just as important as the bigger ones. It's arguably *more* important because the smaller ones happen more frequently and deliver similar rewards. They build your confidence, boost your motivation, and make you feel more engaged. They also trigger the release of dopamine. When this "feel-good" neurotransmitter travels along the neural pathways in your brain, you feel satisfied and fulfilled.

The biggest obstacle that prevents you from experiencing these effects is being in a constant rush. Your attentional resources are fixated on the next thing when you're always on the go. They're consumed by what you should be doing next rather than the small milestones you've achieved.

When you slow down, you can appreciate the progress you've made. You get to celebrate the tiny breakthroughs you've accomplished — breakthroughs without which it would be impossible to achieve your larger goals. Recognizing these small steps forward will not only boost your confidence, motivation, and engagement, but it'll also lift your spirits and increase your joy.

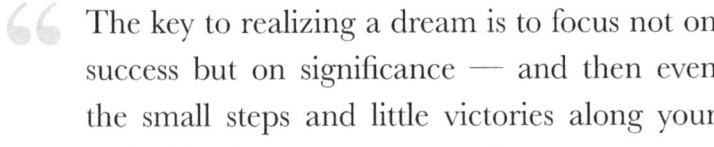 The key to realizing a dream is to focus not on success but on significance — and then even the small steps and little victories along your path will take on greater meaning.

— OPRAH WINFREY

Embrace Moments of Happiness

Sometimes, it feels as though unhappiness has become the new standard. As you rush around trying to do more, see more, and experience more, an undercurrent of stress and anxiety builds. You might not notice it because of your hectic schedule. But it takes a toll on your spirit nonetheless. The stress piles up and eventually feels overwhelming, even if you cannot pinpoint what's causing it.

This is the cost of living in a perpetual state of hustle and grind. You don't have a chance to breathe and reflect. You don't have an opportunity to appreciate the present. You miss the small moments of happiness shaping your joy and contentment.

These moments happen every day. They arise from the small victories you experience, your gratifying interpersonal interactions, and the simple things that always bring you joy (more on this below). These moments go unnoticed and unappreciated when you're always on the go.

Slowing down gives you a chance to embrace these moments as they happen. Instead of rushing to the next thing, you give yourself permission to pause, breathe, and live in the here and now. You get to relish the circumstances that bring you joy *as they occur* rather than promise you'll appreciate them later (a promise likely to be broken).

 Life is all memory, except for the one present moment that goes by you so quickly you hardly catch it going.

— TENNESSEE WILLIAMS

Enjoy Simple Pleasures

Life offers you simple pleasures every day. The problem is that they're easy to miss. Some of these simple pleasures are part of your daily routine. The first sip of coffee in the morning, a hug from your spouse, a home-cooked dinner. They're part of an established pattern and, therefore, seem unremarkable.

Some occur outside your daily routine: a leisurely walk to your favorite store, a gorgeous sunrise you rarely witness, or an opportunity to show kindness and compassion to a stranger in need. They happen sporadically — sometimes inspired and sometimes the result of serendipity.

When you speed through life, preoccupied with staying busy and accomplishing more, there's no time to cherish these small, everyday delights. There's no time to revel in these simple joys that happen each day — simple joys that you can *make* happen each day.

Most people think joy and fulfillment stem from experiencing large-scale thrills and accomplishing huge goals. But in fact, they spring from simple pleasures enjoyed regularly. For example, a long, hot shower on a cold morning. Lounging under a comfortable blanket with a good book. Paying someone a genuine, unexpected compliment and watching their reaction. When you slow things down, you get to savor these everyday joys and humble comforts.

You free yourself to design a life of joy and fulfillment.

> Today, I choose awareness. I choose to be aware of the beauty of life and living. I choose to be aware of the simple pleasures in life. I choose awareness of joy, awareness of peace, and awareness of love.

— IYANLA VANZANT

TOP 5 MISCONCEPTIONS ABOUT GOING SLOW

> Slow living isn't about determining how little we can live with – it's about working out what we simply can't live without.
>
> — NATHAN WILLIAMS

Transitioning from an always-on-the-go way of life to an intentionally, *mindfully* slower pace isn't easy. After years of working hard, the rise-and-grind ethos is likely baked into your state of mind. It has become second nature. Unraveling this mindset, reconditioning your way of thinking, and curbing the hustle-and-bustle habit takes time.

But another obstacle stands in your way, and it's a big one. The notion of living a slower-paced life is linked to several fallacies. These misconceptions about slowing down carry an air of shame and guilt. They can cause you to feel as though you're not living up to your potential. That you're falling short in some way. That you're under-achieving and, therefore, missing out on what life has to offer.

Below, as we dissect the most common misunderstand-ings about going slow, you'll see that the opposite is true. By slowing down, you're neither limiting yourself nor missing out. Instead, you can finally pursue what's impor-tant to you and capitalize on life's rich possibilities.

Myth #1: Going Slow Is Boring

This fallacy stems from the illusion that being busy *isn't* dull. That rushing around and constantly being on the go is somehow exciting. This fast-paced lifestyle, which encourages a perpetual hustle and bustle, can feel invigo-rating in the moment.

But it's a mirage. The sense of excitement springs from an undercurrent of stress, anxiety, and fear. When you're constantly hustling and grinding, you don't feel engaged or interested as much as spurred by a meaningless compulsion to do more.

When you slow down, you develop and savor deeper connections with friends and loved ones. You delight in the simple pleasures that make life truly rewarding. You invest your time and energy in hobbies that bring you genuine fulfillment. These are not the hallmarks of a boring life.

On the contrary, they are the ingredients of a life lived well.

 We're a species that rushes through everything, then complains that time flies.

— STEVE MARABOLI

Myth # 2: Going Slow Is Lazy

Hustle culture has become so ingrained in society that going slow is associated with laziness. When we see someone embracing a slower-paced lifestyle, we assume they're unmotivated and apathetic. We jump to the conclusion that they must lack goals, shirk their responsibilities and obligations, and be unproductive.

These snap judgments are unfair, uninformed, and often mistaken. Adopting a slower lifestyle has nothing to do with laziness. Instead, the purpose is to ensure that you're investing your time and effort into things that are important to you. Instead of dashing about, struggling to juggle more balls than you can reasonably manage, you focus on the few that deliver the greatest impact.

When you commit to slowing down, you're not being lazy. You're being intentional. You're mindful of how you spend your limited resources, including time, attention, energy, and money. You're being *purposeful*.

Slow down and enjoy life. It's not only the scenery you miss by going too fast – you also miss the sense of where you are going and why.

— EDDIE CANTOR

Myth #3: Going Slow Means Abandoning Your Goals

Goal achievement has been wrongly tied to the rise-and-grind work ethic. Many people assume that being in a constant state of activity brings you closer to success. That simply being in motion is a prerequisite for accomplishing things.

This misguided and shortsighted mindset reinforces today's obsession with the always-on-the-go lifestyle. It bolsters the wrongheaded notion that slowing down means giving up on what you want to achieve.

But in fact, slowing down has the opposite effect. It sharpens your focus, encouraging you to reassess which of your goals are truly important to you. It recognizes that your time, energy, and other attentional resources are limited and should be spent where they'll have the most significant impact. It prevents you from spreading yourself too thinly, a circumstance more likely to result in failure and frustration than success.

Let go of the idea that the more you strive, the more you'll accomplish. In reality, achieving your most important goals is often a matter of eliminating the unimportant ones.

 Things which matter most must never be at the mercy of things which matter least.

— JOHANN WOLFGANG VON GOETHE

Myth #4: You Don't Have the Freedom to Slow Down

This fallacy is arguably one of the most tragic. An unhurried life is commonly dismissed as a manner reserved for the fortunate few. Those who have money. Those who have neither responsibilities nor obligations. The affluent. The privileged. The elite.

This assumption discourages people from imagining a slower-paced, peaceful life. They believe that staying relentlessly busy is the only way to stay afloat. They feel overextended and burnt out but can't conceive of going slower because they lack time, money, or other resources.

This state of mind often springs from a faulty premise. It's easy to grow so accustomed to a way of living that it seems like your only option. The hustle and bustle of your daily routine becomes so ingrained that you believe there's no way you can slow down. You don't have the luxury. You start to feel that slowing down will cause your life to crumble.

But this presumption is almost always wrong. In truth, nearly all of us take on more than we need to. We take on more than we're required to. We say "yes" when we should say "no." This tendency can reach the point that constantly rushing around seems normal. It seems *necessary*. It seems *vital*. But once you trim your life of the unessential, this fallacy implodes. When it does so, you'll see you have more freedom than you imagined.

> Most people fail in life because they major in minor things.
>
> — TONY ROBBINS

Myth #5: You'll Miss Out If You Slow Down

By this point, you've undoubtedly noticed a common theme in these misconceptions. Embracing a slower pace doesn't mean you'll miss out. Nor does it mean you have to forfeit opportunities and experiences that are important to you. In fact, the opposite is true. When you slow down, you miss *fewer* of these things.

The greatest irony of speeding through life is that doing so prevents you from enjoying the richness of it. You're doing all the things. You're meeting all the people. You're experiencing all the moments. But in the process, you're robbing yourself of the opportunity to do the things that genuinely gratify you. For example, meeting the people who'll broaden your horizons, challenge you, and elevate your spirits. Experiencing the moments that will genuinely make your life more rewarding.

When you embrace the idea of slowing down and living more intentionally, you abandon the fear of missing out (FOMO). The anxiety that you're overlooking possibilities or passing up opportunities dissipates. This fear eventually goes away entirely and no longer has a hold on you. In its absence, you have the time and energy to pursue what matters most to you. You have the time and energy to design a genuinely fulfilling life.

 Life is too important to waste on speed.

— MILAN KUNDERA

We covered a lot of ground in Part I. We addressed the biggest issues associated with hustle culture and made a compelling case for taking a different path. In Part II, I'll walk you through a step-by-step process for embracing a slower-paced lifestyle and ensuring it sticks.

PART II

MASTER THE ART OF GOING SLOW

∾

Our culture applauds winning. The bigger the win, the bigger the celebration. So naturally, everything becomes a competition.

We compete against coworkers to garner praise, promotions, and raises. We compete against fellow students, attempting to gain the favor of our professors. We compete against friends, striving to outdo them in various inconsequential ways. We compete against ourselves, pursuing goals that only grow more challenging with time. We compete against the clock, trying desperately to get more done during our day.

This constant attention to winning reinforces the

hustle-and-grind state of mind. Worse, the longer you devote yourself to it, the harder it becomes to let it go.

It turns into an obsession.

Making matters worse, the clamor and chaos that accompany an always-on-the-go lifestyle deters you from asking why. Both distract you from reflecting on whether you feel satisfied or are just spinning your wheels. They prevent you from recognizing that you're struggling to keep an unsustainable pace and that burnout is in your future unless you make a change.

Let's make that change. Let's decelerate and create new habits and routines that focus on what is most important to you.

Let's master the art of going slow.

STEP 1: REFLECT ON YOUR NATURE

> What lies behind us and what lies before us are
> tiny matters compared to what lies within us.

— RALPH WALDO EMERSON

Many of our behaviors are on autopilot. They arise from years of mental conditioning and now occur without our thinking about them. Sometimes, they're rooted in habits, routines, and thought patterns that we cultivate from an early age. Other times, they're triggered by cues — both internal and external — that have developed as a result of past experiences.

By the time we reach adulthood, our behaviors and mindset are deeply ingrained. They've become a part of our instinct. We act, react, and associate reflexively rather than after careful consideration.

Sometimes, this works to our benefit. The brain can recognize situational cues and evoke relevant and suitable responses without wasting time and energy. But it can also work to our detriment. We end up behaving in unhealthy ways without knowing the reason. And because we do so on autopilot, we're rarely compelled to uncover the triggers.

The first step toward adopting a slower-paced lifestyle is to figure out why you're rushing to begin with.

Identify the Cues That Cause You to Rush

The compulsion to continuously stay busy can be traced back to many potential factors. These can include your upbringing, self-image, and various fears you've developed. They can involve feelings of obligation, concerns about missing out, and misunderstandings about success. The compulsion to always be on the go might emanate from years of practice; you might live a frantic, perpetually busy lifestyle simply because you've always done so. Old habits die hard.

Whatever the root causes, you've likely indulged — and consequently reinforced — the compulsion without realizing it. You'll need to identify your personal cues to manage and eventually overcome that impulse.

This can only occur through self-awareness stimulated by self-reflection. Fair warning: it can be uncomfortable.

After all, part of the process involves identifying and owning your weaknesses. But the upside is that you'll gain insight into your motives, fears, values, and emotions and how they spur you to constantly stay busy.

How to Self Reflect

Self-reflection entails more than just sitting down and contemplating what makes you tick. You'll be examining your mindset, thought patterns, and motivations. Assessing your attitude and disposition. Questioning your assumptions regarding what defines success, contentment, and happiness *for you*. You'll get the best results by being methodical.

First, determine what you want to discover about yourself. It's easy to get lost in the weeds, letting your mind wander from one aspect of your life to another. Focus on a solitary purpose: learning why you're always in a hurry. Commit to resolving this particular challenge and excluding all other issues.

Second, brainstorm a small list of specific questions to help you identify your triggers. Some of these questions should serve as prompts that inspire a deeper investigation of your thought processes. Your list should be unique to your circumstances, priorities, and disposition. Here are a few sample questions to help you get started:

- What are my core values and principles?

- Am I performing tasks that support these values and principles when I'm in a rush?
- What three things matter most to me?
- Am I performing tasks related to these three things when I'm in a rush?
- Is my compulsion to hurry fueled by legitimate responsibilities, or do unfair expectations drive it — from myself and others?
- Is my reason for rushing justified (e.g., trying to meet an important deadline), or is it rooted in my psyche (e.g., discomfort with being inactive?)
- What did I do this week that gave me a feeling of genuine, lasting satisfaction?
- What did I do this week that left me emotionally exhausted and empty?
- What worries do I have? What provokes them?

Again, these questions are merely a starting point. Use them as inspiration to develop a list that reflects *your* life conditions. I recommend writing your questions down so they're in front of you. That way, you can reflect on them without losing your focus.

The third step is to write down your answers. Doing so will make it easier to compose and organize your thoughts. Moreover, it'll allow you to review your answers down the road, noting changes in your circumstances, priorities, and attitude.

You'll find that answering one question will often lead to other questions. Go with the flow as long as they relate to your solitary purpose. If your mind begins to entertain questions that have nothing to do with discovering why you're always on the go, ignore them.

I've found that the best way to record answers to self-reflection questions is to write them in a journal.

Record Your Thoughts in a Journal

Journaling will help you unearth thoughts, beliefs, and emotions buried under a mountain of psychological conditioning. Once they're unearthed, you can review them objectively, discovering who you are and what is important to you.

Journaling encourages you to scrutinize your ideas and assumptions without fear of judgment or rejection. You can express your concerns and anxieties knowing you'll be the only one to read them. You can examine your shortcomings (real or perceived), brainstorm potential solutions to overcome them, and track your results when you implement those solutions. When you journal, you allow your inner voice to articulate your priorities.

If you've never kept a journal, you may be unsure how to do it effectively. Here are a few tips to get you started.

1. Be mindful of the type of journaling you're about to do. There are many types, and each one has a specific purpose. They include gratitude journaling, goal journaling, vision

journaling, and dream journaling (to name a few). You'll be doing reflective journaling.

2. Commit to setting aside judgments. You must be able to write down your thoughts without your inner critic convincing you that they're silly, stupid, or shameful.

3. Have your list of self-reflection questions in front of you. These questions will be your journaling prompts. They'll keep you focused on what you're trying to accomplish.

4. Schedule your journaling sessions. I recommend practicing reflective journaling once each week. Choose a day when you have 30 minutes of free time and privacy. Create time blocks for your sessions and put them on your calendar.

5. You can write in a paper-based journal or write in digital form. Choose a method and stick with it. I recommend using a cloud-based platform (e.g., Google Docs) if you write in digital form. That way, you can retrieve and review your entries on multiple devices.

6. Promise yourself that you'll be honest. There's no value to reflective journaling unless your answers are truthful. Be candid and sincere. Be authentic. Remember, your journal entries are for your eyes only. No one else is going to read them. So, you may as well be forthright.

We've covered a lot of material in this chapter. Let's do a quick exercise that puts it to practical use.

EXERCISE #1

THIS EXERCISE IS best done when you catch yourself rushing around. Grab a pen and a piece of paper. Find a quiet space in your home. Prepare to use the "5 Whys." This is a simple technique that'll help you to uncover your root motivations.

First, ask yourself why you're rushing. You probably have a specific reason. We'll learn whether that reason is justified during this exercise.

Then, drill down on your first response by asking yourself a series of subsequent "whys."*

For example, suppose you find yourself rushing around on the weekend. Here's how a "5 Whys" conversation with yourself might evolve:

Why am I rushing around?

> I'm trying to complete a mile-long to-do list.

---

* Although this root cause analysis is called "The 5 Whys," you can use more or fewer than five.

Why do I have a mile-long to-do list?

There are a lot of tasks I need to do for my family.

Why do I need to do so many tasks for my family?

If I don't do these tasks, they won't get done.

Why won't these tasks get done if I don't do them?

No one else in my family will do them.

Why won't anyone else in my family do them?

Everyone expects me to do them.

Why does everyone expect me to do them?

I've always done them.

Now, we're getting to the heart of the matter. Your impulse to hurry in this example is spurred by others' expectations, fueled by an established routine.

Are those expectations fair? Is the current routine your only option? Or can you replace it with one that delegates tasks to select family members? Now is also the time to ask yourself if every task on your to-do list is worth spending time and energy on. Can you let some of the items go without consequence?

I recommend writing down this conversation in your self-reflection journal. Not only will doing so help you to focus, but you'll be able to return to it anytime you desire.

Time required: 20 minutes

STEP 2: EXAMINE YOUR GOALS AND INTERESTS

❝ Slow down and enjoy life. It's not only the scenery you miss by going too fast - you also miss the sense of where you are going and why.

— EDDIE CANTOR

We've mentioned goals in passing. Because they are crucial in determining how you spend your time, energy, and attention, we need to explore them in greater detail.

Several aspects of goal setting and goal achievement shape who you are and influence what you do (and how you do it). If you want to adopt a slower-paced lifestyle, you must understand these aspects as they apply to your everyday activities.

In addition to your goals, you have a palate of interests. You have hobbies and pastimes. Some of these have a specific purpose — they help you to relax, stay in shape, express yourself, or give you a sense of accomplishment. Some have no purpose beyond simple enjoyment; you practice them because doing so gives you satisfaction.

Like goal setting and goal achievement, your avocations reflect who you are and inform what you do. But they are a counterpoint to the former. While your goals compel you to rush and grind, your interests encourage you to slow down and savor the present.

Below, we'll explore both sides of this coin. We'll create lists of your goals and interests and then prioritize both. This process will reveal which activities improve your quality of life and which undermine it.

Identify Your Goals

It's tempting to think of your goals as a single, consolidated whole. However, many goals are tied to different aspects of your life. Before you can prioritize them, you must identify them. Here are the main categories that goals fall into:

- Health and fitness
- Personal development
- Skill development
- Career
- Education

- Financial
- Relationships
- Lifestyle
- Spirituality

It's also tempting to blur the line between goals and wishful thinking. For example, suppose you'd like to purchase your first home. That's a practical goal. You can determine the specific steps you'll need to take and the sacrifices you'll need to make to achieve that outcome.

On the other hand, suppose you want to quit your job and become a chart-topping, world-renowned musician with a lucrative recording deal. This outcome may be possible, but it's impractical. The steps to achieve it are obscure, and the competition is intense.

With this in mind, reflect on your goals. Ask yourself what you want to accomplish in each of the above categories. Because specificity is vital to achieving goals, ask yourself what date you'd like to accomplish these things. Put these items in list form, and then set the list aside.

I recommend doing this digitally, either in a text document or spreadsheet. That way, you can easily add and remove items and adjust their target dates.

Identify Your Passions

"Passions" is a strong word. But in the context of identifying hobbies, interests, and activities that improve your quality of life, we use it appropriately.

These are the pursuits that fill you with joy and get you excited. You feel wholly engaged while doing them. You lose track of time because you become immersed in them. They're the seeds of your identity and personality and can reveal your character, values, and beliefs. They might even give your life meaning and purpose.

Your passions make life worth living.

Surprisingly, many people can't articulate the hobbies and interests they're passionate about. They've never taken the time to identify with them. They enjoy doing them but rarely experience the deep-seated enthusiasm and self-motivation normally associated with them. The problem is that these pursuits are easily abandoned as unimportant without this emotional connection.

Instead of making life worth living, they're sacrificed to get more done or chase new things (i.e., shiny object syndrome). Rather than encouraging a slower, more mindful, and intentional pace, they're cast aside in favor of more rushing, hustling, and grinding.

For this reason, you must identify your passions. You must be able to describe the hobbies, interests, and activities with which you feel an emotional connection.

Reflect on the pursuits that bring you a genuine sense of joy. This goes beyond streaming your favorite television shows or spending time with friends. These are the interests in which you're fully invested and engaged when you do them. You daydream about them when you're *not* doing them. You set aside time each week — or each day — to do them. You share them with your friends and loved ones and encourage them to participate.

These are the things that add depth and purpose to your life. They make your life meaningful.

Write them down.

I recommend identifying your goals digitally, as this will make the next step easier.

Prioritize Your Goals and Interests

You've listed your goals. You've listed your interests. It's time to rank them in order of importance to you.

Every goal and interest requires your time, energy, and attention. The challenge is that all three of these are limited resources. You lack time, energy, and attention to accomplish every goal and pursue every interest. So you must spend these resources wisely, in a manner that makes the best use of them.

Only you can determine how to do this. Only you can decide which of your goals take priority over the rest. Only you can choose which of your hobbies and passions hold greater value than the others.

Start prioritizing the items on each of your lists by putting them in one of two categories:

1. Non-negotiable
2. Desirable but not vital

The first category contains the goals and interests you

can't live without. These might include saving for retirement, getting married and having kids, earning a doctorate, or starting a business. They can include hobbies such as travel, painting, and volunteer work. These are the items for which you're willing to forfeit all others.

The second category contains goals and interests you're willing to abandon if you have to. They're important to you, but they're not imperative. You can live without them.

We don't need to prioritize the items in the first category further. The fact that they're "non-negotiable" is enough. However, we need to prioritize the items in the second category further. The best way to do this is by asking yourself a series of self-reflective questions.

For your goals:

- "What happens if I don't achieve this goal?"
- "What happens if I put it on the back burner?"
- "What resources do I need to achieve it?"
- "Do I require others' help to achieve it?"
- "How excited do I feel about achieving it?"
- "Does this goal align with my core values?"
- "What must I sacrifice to achieve it?"

For your interests:

- "How does engaging this interest benefit me?"
- "How do I feel when I'm immersed in it?"
- "How do I feel when I'm *not* immersed in it?"
- "What resources do I need to indulge in it?"

- "Does this interest align with my core values?"
- "What must I forfeit to pursue it?"
- "If I were forced to choose only one interest from this list, would I choose this one?"

This process will reveal where you should spend your time, energy, and attention. It's a crucial step toward embracing a slower pace and optimizing your quality of life.

EXERCISE #2

THIS EXERCISE BUILDS upon the work you did earlier. It'll cast your goals and interests in a different light, showing if your earlier prioritization is accurate. The results will likely validate your choices. On the other hand, you may need to spend more time reflecting on what is truly important to you.

On a piece of paper, create a simple matrix. Draw a vertical line down the left side. Then, starting from the bottom of this line, draw a horizontal line toward the right side. Label the vertical line (the Y axis) "Importance." Label the horizontal line (the X axis) "Satisfaction."

Now, plot each of your goals and interests on your matrix. The position of each dot should reflect how important that item is to you and how much you enjoy pursuing it.

This exercise won't provide concrete answers. That's not its purpose. Instead, it'll help you see your goals and interests from a perspective that adds nuance and depth to your earlier prioritization.

Time required: 15 minutes

STEP 3: DETERMINE HOW YOU CURRENTLY SPEND YOUR TIME

 Doing a huge number of things doesn't mean you're getting anything meaningful done.

— LEO BABAUTA

U nless you've recently tracked your time, there's a good chance you're spending it in ways that will surprise you. If you're not vigilant, time can easily slip through your fingers. You find yourself scrambling to get things done as a regular part of your day.

This can happen when you repeatedly take on favors, tasks, projects, and other commitments that you would rather decline. It can occur as your daily routine becomes bloated with activities that have little value or meaning to you. The former circumstance feeds the latter. Routinely saying "yes" to others causes your calendar and to-do list to become overloaded with items you find unimportant.

Have you ever felt mentally exhausted at the end of your day and at the same time frustrated because you sense that you've made no real progress? If so, you've likely spent your time in a manner that's out of sync with your values, priorities, goals, and interests. Life has surreptitiously filled your schedule to the brim with chores, assignments, and obligations that are neither meaningful nor gratifying to you. This is a form of "task creep."*

To prevent this scenario, you must be keenly aware of how you're spending your time. The best way to do this is to perform a time audit.

How to Perform a Time Audit

A time audit addresses a specific problem: it reconciles how you spend your time with how you *think* you spend your time. The two may be radically different. A time audit will reveal the differences, giving you the insight to make reasonable and informed adjustments.

You can use many methods to perform a time audit, but I recommend following a simple 3-step procedure. The simpler your approach, the less likely you'll get overwhelmed and bogged down by unnecessary minutiae.

---

* Task creep is a nod to "feature creep," a phenomenon that occurs during product development. Features are continually added to a product until it becomes overstuffed with nonessential attributes that diminish its usability.

First, decide how you'll track your time. You can do so digitally or in written form. If you choose to do it digitally, there are countless tools you can use, from spreadsheets to apps. Reliable spreadsheet programs include Google Sheets, Numbers, LibreOffice, and Open Office (all free). Reliable apps include Toggl, RescueTime, Clockify, and Simple Time Tracker (all offer a free option).

I recommend using pen and paper. Doing so requires more effort, but the tactile experience of writing things down brings everything into focus. Create a simple 4-column template in a spreadsheet program. Apply the following column headings (from left to right):

- Start Time
- End Time
- Duration
- Activity

Then, print 14 copies to track your time for two weeks — one sheet per day.

The second step is to track your time. When you begin an activity, note the starting time. When you stop, note the ending time. Then, calculate how much time you spent on it, and describe the activity in a few words.

Some of your activities will be part of your daily routine — for example, reading and responding to email. Use a single word (e.g., "email," "break," etc.) to describe them. Some activities will happen outside your daily routine but occur so frequently that they, too, should be described with a single word (e.g., "meetings," "chores," etc.). The purpose of doing this will become apparent in the third step.

The third step happens after you've tracked your time for 14 days. You're going to analyze your results. First, review each activity that appears on your time tracking sheets and apply one of the following labels to each:

- Non-negotiable
- Optional

Alternatively, you can use two colored pens. Assign the colors based on the above labels, and mark each activity with the appropriate color. Your primary concern is identifying which activities are essential and which aren't.

Next, grab another sheet of paper. Write down the *types* of activities that occupied your time during your 14-day tracking period. This is where your single-word category descriptions will be helpful. Frequently-occurring activities, such as "email," "meetings," "chores," etc., can be placed into a few large buckets. You'll not only save time doing this, but you'll also see how much of your time these bucket activities consume.

Finally, calculate the amount of time you spent on each type of activity (or category). Add the values you recorded in your tracking sheets' "Duration" column. Then, record the *aggregate* values next to the corresponding activity types.

Analyze Your Time Audit Data

You now have the information you need. Let's analyze it and put it to use.

Begin by conducting a high-level overview. Skim your 14 daily tracking sheets and look for inconsistencies between how you spent your time and how you *thought* you spent your time. Did a particular activity monopolize your schedule? Did you take more breaks than you imagined? These data provide a reality check.

Next, note where you spent the majority of your time. Did you spend it doing important tasks that align with your values, responsibilities, goals, and interests? Or did you squander it on trivial distractions and meaningless activities?*

Now, look for clues that reveal changes in your energy levels throughout each day. Are you most productive and enthusiastic during the hours before lunch, after which your energy and focus wane? Or do you tend to drag your feet during these hours and do your best work *after* lunch? Does a particular activity drain your energy and enthusiasm more quickly than others (e.g., meetings)?

Finally, sift through your tracking sheets and look for opportunities to make changes. For example, are there high-priority tasks that you can delegate? Are there low-

---

* This does not include taking breaks. Regular breaks are essential to staying productive, making good decisions, and solving problems.

priority tasks that you can sideline? Are there time-wasters that you can abandon?

The goal is to fill your plate with activities that are meaningful to you. They should either gratify you or fulfill a responsibility that you cannot shirk. The first step is to identify time-sapping activities that have minimal value to you based on the above attributes. Then, look for opportunities to replace them with more enriching activities. You may be surprised by how often this is possible.

Adjust Your Calendar and Schedule

This is simultaneously the most straightforward and most challenging part of the process. Tracking your time is easy. Learning where your activities deviate from your priorities and interests is also easy. However, making changes based on this insight is harder. Not only are some activities unavoidable, but some are linked to longstanding routines.

Our routines become deeply embedded in our minds. The longer we practice them, the more rooted they become. They evolve within habit loops, anchoring and reinforcing existing neural pathways. This is why we find it so challenging to break behavioral patterns that we know are pointless and even detrimental to us.

You'll face this challenge when you adjust how you spend your time. You'll be unraveling ingrained patterns to create new ones. The good news is that you already possess the tools to help you do this.

Recall from Step 2 (the previous chapter) that you identified, listed, and prioritized your goals and interests. And if you did the exercise, you're armed with a plot diagram that gives you a bird's-eye view of how these goals and interests contribute to your quality of life.

Have these tools in front of you. They'll continuously remind you of the day-to-day experience you want to create for yourself. They'll give you the nudge to break well-established routines and form new, more rewarding ones based on your goals and interests.

Can you design a daily schedule filled exclusively with activities that are important to you? Probably not. You have responsibilities. You have obligations. You may have people who depend on you. Unless you're wealthy, you have to be prudent with your money. But you *can* recalibrate how you spend your time, making minor adjustments here and there to make the most of it.

That's crucial to this process: making minor adjustments over the long run. They add up and eventually pay huge dividends. And as your modified routines gain traction, they'll help to "enforce" a slower pace — one that increasingly includes activities that are meaningful to you.

∾

EXERCISE #3

∾

THE PURPOSE of this exercise is to interrupt the mental conditioning that makes your current routines seem indispensable. It gives you a chance to imagine yourself doing what you want rather than what you feel you must do. It also encourages you to scrutinize the latter and ask yourself, "Do I legitimately *need* to do these things?"

First, suppose you have two hours each day to do anything you desire. You can sleep. You can watch your favorite programs on Netflix. You can take leisurely walks, spend time with your family, or write the novel you've always wanted to write. This time is entirely yours.

Write down the first five activities that come to mind. These activities represent a wish list of sorts.

Second, grab the 14 daily tracking sheets you completed during your time audit. Replace two hours of activities on these sheets with the five activities on your wish list.

There's only one rule: you cannot wake up earlier or go to bed later to squeeze more time out of your day. You must *replace* activities. You must abandon things you're currently doing to make room for your "wish list" activities.

Don't worry about whether it's realistic. This visualization exercise is designed to challenge your assumptions.

Time required: 20 minutes

STEP 4: REDUCE YOUR COMMITMENTS

Half of the troubles of this life can be traced to saying yes too quickly and not saying no soon enough.

—JOSH BILLINGS

We make commitments for many reasons, and not all are good. On the positive side, we commit to accomplishing meaningful goals, adopting healthy habits and productive routines, standing by our values and convictions, and building trust with others. These reasons are commendable and inspire us to design a lifestyle that dovetails with our principles, priorities, and aspirations.

On the negative side, we often pledge to do things for

unhealthy and self-sabotaging reasons. For example, many of us have been conditioned from childhood to believe that making a commitment is intrinsically honorable and virtuous. That the act itself is noble and praiseworthy. This cognitive programming often compels us to commit to the wrong things.

An example of this behavior is the unwillingness to say "no" to people. We commit to doing favors, working on projects, and attending events that we'd rather not do, work on, or attend. Saying "yes" becomes a habit, and we end up *overcommitting*. We find ourselves rushing around to do things for others instead of addressing our own needs and interests. In so doing, we compromise our happiness and ultimately undermine our quality of life.

If you'd like to embrace a slower-paced lifestyle, you must first review your current commitments. They may seem inflexible. But some of them may be less binding than you believe. Once you've reviewed them objectively, you can decide which ones to keep and which to withdraw from. You can then focus on developing habits that will shield you from overcommitment in the future.

Let's do a deep dive into this process now.

Evaluate Your Commitments

In *Step 2: Examine Your Goals and Interests*, you created two lists. One list featured your goals, and the other featured your passions. In *Step 3: Determine How You Currently Spend Your Time*, we noted that you have responsibilities you can't avoid. You also performed a two-week time audit, which resulted in 14 daily tracking sheets.

You'll now use these tools to gauge whether you're devoting your time, attention, and energy as you should. They will help you determine if you're committed to the right things. They'll highlight favors, projects, and roles you've pledged yourself to that might be good candidates for the chopping block.

Draw a line down the middle of a sheet of paper. On the left side, write down all of your commitments. You'll find much of this information on your 14 daily tracking sheets. You may need to mull over commitments that don't happen daily (e.g., paying bills, meeting a particular friend for lunch once a month, etc.). These may not appear on your tracking sheets but warrant your attention nonetheless.

On the right side of the line, create two columns. In the first column, assign a value from 1 to 10 for each commitment you've written down. The values you assign will represent how your commitments align with your goals and passions.

In the second column, answer a simple question with "yes" or "no":

"Can I step away from this?"

Don't worry about how you might step away from it (i.e., delegating it, sidelining it, or abandoning it). Concern yourself only with whether you *can*.

Once you've filled out your sheet of paper, it'll contain helpful information that wasn't previously apparent to you. You'll likely notice that some of your commitments aren't as important as you thought. You may also discover that some aren't nearly as binding as you thought.

Let Go of Optional, Unimportant Commitments

You've done the heavy lifting. You've scrutinized your commitments with the intent to renounce those that are needlessly and wastefully monopolizing your time, attention, and energy. It's now time to take action on your newfound insight. It's time to let go of some of your commitments.

This is easier said than done for three reasons:

1. Our routines become part of our identity
2. Letting go feels as though we're letting people down and disappointing them
3. It feels dishonorable and unprincipled

These reasons are anchored in our thought patterns, which emanate from our cognitive programming. Overcoming this conditioning is no simple matter. But it's doable with a few practical tips and consistent practice.

First, recognize that few commitments are permanent. They might *feel* permanent because of the significance you've attached to them. But few last forever. Once you embrace this truth, you'll begin to view your commitments through a different lens that isn't steeped in guilt, shame, or anxiety.

Second, acknowledge that you're not obligated to meet others' expectations. While some of your commitments are impossible to walk away from while simultaneously being shaped by others' expectations (e.g., providing shelter and food for your kids), those expectations have little to do with your commitment. In these cases, you don't remain committed to appease others; you stay committed because you're compelled to act according to your values and principles, which inform your sense of responsibility. This is a critical distinction.

Third, come up with a respectful, diplomatic way to communicate your intention to walk away from an optional commitment. Simply telling someone, "I'm not doing this anymore!" won't suffice. It expresses your intention but will likely damage your reputation, hurt your credibility, and cause needless resentment.

Tact and grace will go a long way toward avoiding unnecessary conflict. Here are a few suggestions:

- Be upfront about your intention. Don't try to hide it or dance around it. Candor is difficult but usually respected.
- Offer a brief explanation. Don't feel obligated to give a lengthy justification for your decision. Clarity and brevity are essential.
- Acknowledge that your decision might

disappoint or displease the person you're talking to.

- Be assertive if the person you're talking to pushes back. Stand your ground. Remember, being assertive doesn't mean being combative. You can be assertive, respectful, and kind at the same time.

These tips will make withdrawing from commitments that aren't set in stone easier. But we're not done. There's one more step you can take to avoid overcommitment: steering clear of *new* commitments that are optional and unimportant to you.

Say "No" More Often

If you want to lead a life free of unnecessary commitments and superfluous responsibilities, saying "no" is the most useful habit you can adopt. This single practice, when done consistently, will shield you from needless stress and anxiety. It'll help you focus on your needs, goals, and interests instead of constantly rushing to appease others.

Numerous things can contribute to feeling overcommitted and overwhelmed, and some may not be obvious. Consider saying no to the following:

- tasks that are not your responsibility
- meetings that are unrelated to your projects
- favors that you're uncomfortable doing

- favors that require too much of your time
- social engagements that are unimportant to you
- unnecessary interruptions
- meaningless distractions
- waiting around for people
- gossip

Some of the above may seem small and inconsequential in how they affect your day. You may feel that you can attend to them without becoming overcommitted. But therein lies their capacity to overwhelm. It's easy to underestimate their impact and allow them to drain your limited time, energy, and attention. As you start to say no more consistently, it'll become more evident how much of these precious resources they consume.

Saying no isn't easy. If you're a chronic people pleaser, saying no will oppose your natural tendencies. Here are a few tips that will make doing so easier:

- Be clear and concise
- Be tactful and respectful
- Offer a *brief* explanation
- Don't apologize
- Be assertive when you encounter pushback
- Suggest an alternative solution

If saying no feels uncomfortable, don't despair. As with adopting any new habit, this one becomes easier with practice. And if your normal day-to-day is typical, you'll have countless opportunities to practice, refine, and eventually master this skill.

Speaking of getting some practice, let's do a quick exercise.

~

EXERCISE #4

~

FOR THIS EXERCISE, we'll use the multi-column sheet you created above. Recall that you answered a simple question for each of your commitments:

"Can I step away from this?"

Look at the commitments for which you answered "yes." These are the non-binding activities from which you can distance yourself. Review the values (i.e., 1 through 10) you assigned to these commitments. Choose the one with the lowest value.

Now, create a "walk away" plan. Write down the steps you'll take to disengage from this activity. Depending on the commitment, this may be as simple as no longer doing it.

For example, suppose you're committed to responding immediately to emails. You check for new emails dozens of times each day to maintain this practice. You can choose to no longer do this without seeking permission from others or delegating the task. Moreover, you might decide to do it on the spot rather than over an extended period, which would preclude creating a timeline for your "walk away" plan.

If the commitment you've chosen for this exercise is more entangling, your "walk away" plan will be more elaborate. Other people may be involved. The activity may need to be performed, but no one is trained to do it in your stead. Stepping away may require several days, weeks, or months.

For this type of commitment, outline your strategy step by step. Write down the names of people you'll need to talk to, negotiate with, or train. Write down the things that need to happen or the conditions that must be met before you can walk away. Then, given these considerations, choose a reasonable target date by which you'll disengage from the commitment.

Don't worry about whether your "walk away" plan will happen exactly as you've envisioned. For now, *create* the plan. Worry about execution later.

Time required: 30 minutes

STEP 5: PRACTICE CALMING ACTIVITIES

66 In an age of speed, I began to think, nothing
could be more invigorating than going slow.

— PICO IYER

I f you're living a rise-and-grind lifestyle, you're
probably not taking the time to relax and recharge.
At least not as much as you should. You likely feel
you have neither the freedom nor latitude to do so. You
recognize that it's crucial for your mental and emotional
health, but a variety of fears and pressures keep you
hustling.

For example, maybe you fear falling behind on your goals,
so you keep pushing yourself to do more. Or perhaps you fear
missing out on opportunities, any of which you worry might

be the one that will "change everything" for the better. Or maybe you believe your quality of life should be sacrificed on the altar of perpetual productivity. Perhaps you're not great at setting boundaries — in your personal and professional life.

Whatever your motivations, they're pushing you toward burnout and its attendant side effects. If you want to embrace a slower-paced life, live mindfully, and savor the present moment, you must neutralize them.

It won't be easy. It will require patience. These impulses likely formed long ago and have only grown more entrenched with time. But the sooner you start deconstructing them, the sooner you can abandon the hustle and grind of society's high-pressure, always-do-more ethos.

The best way to mitigate these impulses is to regularly perform activities that dampen (and even silence) your mental noise.

10 Activities That Will Quiet Your Mind

Left to its own devices, your mind will occupy itself by worrying and overthinking. It will race with thoughts regarding circumstances you cannot control. It will cause you to fret about financial woes, workplace conflicts, health concerns, and events that have minimal impact on you. It may even seem as though your brain *prefers* the chaos of constant mental noise.

It won't stop on its own. It won't turn itself off. You'll need to take steps to help your brain to unwind. Here are ten simple activities that will replace the mental chatter in your mind with peace and quiet:

1. **Meditation** - a few minutes spent breathing deeply with your eyes closed will calm your mind and give you clarity.
2. **Leisure reading** - find a distraction-free area and enjoy a novel in your favorite genre. Train your brain to immerse itself in the story rather than in pointless worries.
3. **Exercise** - any aerobic activity will suffice. A few minutes of intense exercise will release endorphins that relieve mental clutter.
4. **Journaling** - writing down your thoughts is like relieving a cognitive pressure valve. The more pressure you release, the less inner chatter.
5. **Listening to music** - slow-tempo music (approximately 60 beats per minute) stimulates alpha brainwaves. These brainwaves can put you in a meditative state.
6. **Gardening** - even caring for a single houseplant can help silence the mental noise. Your attention focuses on the present moment as you connect with nature.
7. **Cooking** - you're in complete control. You can immerse yourself and enjoy the process without knowing how to cook.

8. **Walking in nature** - a slow walk on a hiking trail or through a wooded park is mentally soothing. Being surrounded by nature will help you to feel calm and grounded.

9. **Playing with your pet** - this releases serotonin, your body's "feel-good" chemical. You'll feel calmer, happier, and less stressed. (And your pet will love you for it.)

10. **Doing puzzles** - any puzzle will do (jigsaw, crossword, Soduku, etc.). Your brain busies itself looking for patterns, which distracts it from worrying.

These are merely suggestions to help you get started. Countless other activities can quiet your mind. You probably have one or more hobbies you're fond of (e.g., stamp collecting, playing chess, coloring, etc.). Start there and experiment.

One word of caution: I recommend that you avoid social media, YouTube, and TikTok. These platforms are designed to stimulate repeated surges of dopamine. These surges may seem calming at first because they give you an immediate sense of pleasure. But over time, they produce and reinforce addictive behavior.

Create a Quick & Simple Calming Routine

You now have several self-soothing activities that you can perform to calm your mind and help you adopt a slower pace. The important thing is that you perform them *regularly*. Preferably daily.

This is easier said than done, especially if busyness is the norm of your day. Self-care is probably the furthest thing from your mind when you're rushing around, attending to your responsibilities, meeting deadlines, and putting out fires. Most people neglect self-care not because it's difficult but because the commotion and chaos of life get in the way.

So, you'll need to take purposeful action to make it happen. The most effective strategy I've found is to establish a calming routine and follow it at a scheduled time each day.

First, choose a time that's ideal for you. Take into account your daily schedule, commitments, chores, and energy levels. For example, suppose you work 8:00 a.m. to 6:00 p.m., have chores or errands to run afterward, and are usually exhausted when you finish them. In this case, you might perform your calming routine from 6:30 a.m. to 7:00 a.m. On the other hand, if you work from home and have a flexible schedule, you might do it right after lunch.

Second, string multiple activities into a sequence instead of relying on a single activity. Doing this has two benefits. First, going through the sequence will keep your mind occupied, distracting it from worrying and overthinking. Second, it'll allow you to monitor which activities produce the best outcome. A 30-minute calming routine might involve five or six activities.

Third, schedule your routine on your daily calendar.

Block off time and treat it like an appointment. This will encourage you to follow it daily, and eventually, it will become an enduring habit.

Ideally, you can go through your calming routine whenever you feel stressed and overwhelmed. It might not be feasible to drop everything and perform your *entire* routine. But you may be able to unplug for five minutes and do one or two of your chosen activities. This is another benefit of having several at your fingertips.

EXERCISE #5

THE PURPOSE of this exercise is to evaluate several self-soothing activities and note how they make you feel as you're doing them. Some will be more calming than others.

You've (hopefully) created a list of activities that you enjoy doing and make you feel relaxed and at peace. If you haven't written them down, do so now.

Next, perform each activity on your list. Ten minutes should suffice for each one. Observe your thoughts, headspace, and emotional state while doing them. Do they distract your mind from the chaos of your day? Do you enter a flow state where the rest of the world fades into the background? Or is doing the activity fruitless?

Rate each activity on your list from 1 to 10. This rating will indicate how effective the activity is in calming your mind. Build your calming routine using the activities you've rated the highest.

Time required: 60 minutes

STEP 6: ADOPT A "SLOW LIVING" HABIT

> Sow a thought, and you reap an act; sow an act, and you reap a habit; sow a habit, and you reap a character; sow a character, and you reap a destiny.

— CHARLES READE

Embracing a slower-paced lifestyle requires a shift in mindset. It involves more than just doing things that are calming and soothing. It calls for adjusting your outlook (perhaps radically) and viewing your life in the context of what you can't—or won't—live without.

Adopting this frame of mind is a gradual process. It doesn't happen overnight. It begins when you commit to slowing down, and your mental framework changes over time. Making this commitment is the first vital step. You've planted a seed. What you do afterward will determine whether that seed takes root and bears fruit.

The best way to ensure that this seed flourishes is to develop a "slow living" habit. This involves doing activities that are in sync with a slower-pace lifestyle. But you won't be doing them just for the sake of doing them. Instead, you'll be doing so to internalize and reinforce your new mindset.

Let's start by exploring a few simple practices you can implement into your day that will streamline this process.

10 Practical Ways to Incorporate Slow Living Into Your Mental Framework

In Step 5, we covered ten calming activities to help quiet the noise in your mind. The following ten practices differ not only in purpose but also in their depth of influence. Whereas the calming activities provide short-term relief, these practices are designed to produce a long-term outcome: a fundamental change in how you approach your day.

1. **Turn down requests.** We touched on this in Step 4. Saying "no" is a great way to avoid taking on unnecessary commitments. Additionally, the more you do it, the more

comfortable you will become with maintaining your boundaries.

2. **Clear the clutter.** Clutter is distracting. It harms your mental clarity and contributes to cognitive overload. It can make you feel busy, stressed, and overwhelmed. Clearing the clutter clears your mind, which is essential for slowing down.

3. **Limit distractions you control**. Social media, Netflix, email, phone calls, and texts drain your attentional resources and create mental clutter. The good news is that you likely have more control over these things than you imagine, even when they involve your job.

4. **Schedule your phone use**. This is related to #3 but deserves a moment in the spotlight. Your phone is probably one of your biggest distractions. If so, only turn it on during certain times of the day. For example, turn it on after lunch and turn it off after dinner.* Granted, this may be infeasible, depending on your circumstances. Choose a schedule that works for your situation.

5. **Follow a morning routine**. Your morning sets the tone for the rest of your day. If you rush

---

* I turn my phone on at 3:00 p.m. each day and off at 8:00 p.m. It's on for only five hours. I used to think doing this would be impossible, certainly inconvenient. But once it became a habit, I discovered it was easy and surprisingly rewarding.

around after waking up, you'll probably feel rushed in the hours ahead. Create a simple morning routine. Enjoy a leisurely breakfast. Spend 10 minutes stretching. Read a novel. Listen to music. Talk with your spouse for a few minutes. A relaxed, slow-paced morning routine will shape the vibe for the rest of your day.

6. **Eat in peace**. Turn off your phone, move away from your computer, and enjoy your meals in a quiet, distraction-free environment. Eat mindfully and savor your food. This doesn't mean you must eat in solitude. On the contrary, sharing meals with friends and loved ones is one of life's simplest pleasures. Eating in peace, alone or with others, trains your mind to slow down and revel in the present.

7. **Trim your list of friends**. Quality friendships flourish as trust and emotional intimacy between friends grows. But such friendships require a lot of time and energy to nurture. You don't have enough time and energy to do this with everyone you know. Choose five friends and go "all in." Maintaining fewer friendships means you can focus on developing deeper emotional bonds without spreading yourself too thinly.

8. **Spend *quality* time with people**. When you're with a friend or loved one, give that

person your full attention. Listen intently to what they're saying if you're having a conversation. If you're enjoying an activity together (e.g., cooking, exercising, etc.), make the experience about doing it together rather than the activity itself. Connect with your companion rather than just going through the motions with them.

9. **Spend *quality* time with yourself.** Do fun things independently (preferably without relying on your phone). Go on hikes, visit museums, and take short road trips. Journal, paint, and enjoy lunch at your favorite restaurant. When you spend quality time alone, you can reflect and think more deeply without the pressure to entertain. You also recharge and refuel for the quality time you spend with others.

10. **Follow the speed limit.** If you usually drive like you're competing in NASCAR, you may inadvertently reinforce a hustle-and-grind state of mind. When you drive the speed limit, you encourage your mind to adopt a slower pace — a mindset that permeates other areas of your life. You gradually let go of the compulsion to hurry.

These practices are simple. But don't underestimate their far-reaching impact on your thoughts, attitude, and perspective. They can be transformative, reshaping your mindset and influencing your choices and behaviors. Once you've integrated these practices into your habits and routines, they'll become the foundation for building and fine-tuning your slower-paced lifestyle.

Make Small Changes Slowly

There's no rush to adopt the practices above. The secret to making lifestyle changes stick is to make them slowly, ideally one at a time.

I strongly recommend approaching any lifestyle change by taking small steps. Rather than making big changes quickly, an approach that often fails in the long run, go slowly. Give your mind the time it needs to acclimate. Give yourself the time you need to adjust to a new rhythm.

For example, let's say you're committed to spending quality time with the people you love. Don't leap into it by proposing dozens of activities to do with them. Pick *one* person. Choose *one* activity. Propose it. Enjoy the experience. Then do it again.

Let's say you're convinced that the secret to adopting a slower pace is to follow a relaxing, mindful morning routine. Don't dive into a 90-minute routine filled with back-to-back activities. Select *one* activity. Enjoy doing it for 10 minutes. Note how it makes you feel. If it helps your state of mind, do it again the following morning. After a few days, select a second activity (e.g., stretching) and add it to your routine. After a few more days, add a third activity (e.g., reading).

If you take small steps consistently, they will pay massive dividends in the long run. Slow, consistent progress is the secret to making any lasting change in your life.

EXERCISE #6

FOR THIS EXERCISE, you'll experiment with the slow living practices described above and take notes regarding how they make you feel. You don't have to do all of them. Nor do you have to restrict yourself to the ones listed above. Do as many as you like, and feel free to add your own.

First, create a simple chart to track your experiments. You can do this digitally (any spreadsheet program or note-taking app will suffice) or use pen and paper.

Create five columns. Title the first column "Slow Living Practice." Title the second column "Duration." Title the remaining columns 1, 2, and 3. These last three columns will correspond to the following three self-reflection questions:

1. "How did I feel while doing this activity?"
2. "Did this activity improve or worsen my mood after the fact?"
3. "Did this activity make me more inclined to slow down going forward?"

Answer these questions with one or two words. Or use a numbered scale (e.g., 1 to 10) to reflect how an activity affected you — positively or negatively. Doing so will make it easier to evaluate your results after you've completed several experiments. You'll be able to see at a glance which slow-living practices had the most significant impact on you.

Time required: 15 minutes per experiment

STEP 7: SCALE DOWN INCOMING DIGITAL NOISE

 The cost of anything is the amount of life you exchange for it.

— HENRY DAVID THOREAU

Technology is hijacking your mind. You may not notice it. But it's happening. Devices, platforms, and apps are designed to trigger the release of dopamine. You feel happy while using your phone. You feel energized while you're on social media. You feel rewarded after using any of the dozens of apps on your phone, tablet, or laptop.

There's a lot of digital noise that is carefully engineered to keep you engaged and addicted. That's why it's difficult to stop using your favorite devices, platforms, and apps.

And even when you manage to stop, you feel compelled to return and resume using them. This effect is insidious because it has been specially formulated to ensure you're unaware that it is occurring.

This digital noise has another effect. It clutters your headspace with pointless and continuous distractions. It encourages useless drama, meaningless comparisons, and a persistent fear of missing out. Even when you use it for professional purposes, it can become a breeding ground for information overload.

This is the antithesis of enjoying a slow-paced, mindful lifestyle that prioritizes quality over quantity and encourages you to savor the present. It causes you to feel stressed and anxious. It harms your focus and productivity. It can impair your social interactions, undermine your emotional health, and sabotage your sleep quality.

Now that you know it's happening, let's look at how you can scale down this digital noise to mitigate its impact on you.

Use Technology Purposefully

Technology isn't the problem. The problem stems from how we use it.

We have remarkable tools at our disposal. They help us to research topics, solve problems, automate tasks, and optimize processes. They allow us to find people who share our values, collaborate with others to advance shared goals, and connect with people we care about. These tools enable us to track every facet of our personal and professional lives, from our sleep quality and daily routines to our productivity and progress on work-related projects.

But these tools come with temptation. We doomscroll, fixating on negative news. We spend excessive time on social media, chasing the drama of the day. We waste hours each day watching low-value videos on YouTube.

You can't "quit" technology without paying a severe price. But you *can* train yourself to use it purposefully. Here are seven practical tips you can implement today:

1. **Organize your digital life**. Purge files and folders you no longer need. Close accounts you no longer use. Unsubscribe from emails you no longer read. Get rid of digital media that no longer engages you. Clear out photos that are no longer meaningful to you.

2. **Minimize your notifications**. You have more control than you might realize. Your phone allows you to choose which notifications to receive. Access your phone's settings and turn off app-specific alerts that do little more than distract you. Or do what I do: turn all of them off.

3. **Unfollow drama sources**. Avoid Facebook groups, Twitter opinion makers, TikTok influencers, and YouTube content creators who use rage bait to draw attention.

4. **Establish clear digital goals**. Use technology with a specific purpose in mind. Are you researching a particular topic? Are you looking for a unique, inspired solution? Are you attempting to reconnect with a childhood friend? Know what you want to accomplish before going online.

5. **Set recreational times**. Rather than using technology aimlessly when you're bored, set specific times to use it recreationally. For example, you might allow yourself to scroll through your favorite social media personalities' posts for 30 minutes each evening after dinner.

6. **Organize your notes**. If you use an online app to take notes and store documents, take advantage of its tagging feature. Use tags to categorize your notes and documents so you can find them easily. The more quickly you can find them, the less susceptible you'll be to digital distractions.

7. **Create a digital-free zone**. This might be your kitchen table, an easy chair in a guest room, or your patio. When you visit this space, refrain from using your phone, tablet, laptop, and digital watch.

If you incorporate these tips into your day, you'll slowly feel less dependent on your devices and favorite online platforms. The temptation to turn to them whenever you feel bored will gradually disappear.

It'll take time. And you'll need to be vigilant. That's to be expected since you'll likely be unraveling a long-established and deeply-rooted habit. But eventually, the compulsion to doom scroll, follow negative news, and chase pointless drama online will evaporate.

Use Your Phone Intentionally

Your phone is simultaneously your friend and adversary. On the one hand, it can improve your quality of life. It saves you time, helps you stay organized, and puts crucial information at your fingertips when needed. But your phone can also cause anxiety, sleep problems, social isolation, and even depression. Research also suggests that overuse can weaken your ability to store and process information and perform cognitive tasks, such as focusing, thinking, and reading.[*]

So the problem with your phone isn't that you use it. Nor is it that you always have it near you and depend on it. If your phone is harming your quality of life, the problem is related to *how* you use it.

The good news is that you can reap the countless benefits of using your phone without exposing yourself to the

---

[*] Ward AF, Duke K, Gneezy A, Bos MW. Brain drain: The mere presence of one's own smartphone reduces available cognitive capacity. *Journal of the Association for Consumer Research.* 2017;2(2):140-154. doi:10.1086/691462

potential consequences. It's a matter of using your phone intentionally. Here are five quick tips you can implement right now:

1. **Purge pointless apps**. You probably have apps on your phone that you rarely use or use too much. Delete them, or at the very least remove them from your home screen so they no longer distract you.

2. **Scrutinize your motives**. How do you currently use your phone? What are your reasons for using it in this manner? Why are these reasons important to you?

3. **Track your usage**. You need to know how, when, and how much you use your phone to make purposeful adjustments. The only way to know these things is to monitor your usage. Every time you use your phone, write down the time of day, your purpose, and how long you used it.

4. **Pick ten apps**. These apps should improve your quality of life. They might include your calendar, email, and banking app. They might include tools that help you manage your time, reinforce habit development, and support collaboration with your coworkers. Limit yourself to 10. Fewer, if possible.*

---

* If you're interested, my phone's home screen currently displays the

5. **Schedule phone-free times**. Choose specific times during the day to turn off your phone. Put these time chunks on your daily calendar. I recommend starting small (e.g., 15-minute chunks) to wean yourself from your phone. Increase the duration as your willpower grows.

Bonus tip: write down a complete list of the activities you enjoy that don't require your phone. This list will help you resist the temptation to reach for your phone when you can't think of how else to occupy your time. Your list of activities will be unique to you, but here are a few ideas to get you started:

- Cooking
- Journaling
- Hiking
- Drawing
- Napping
- Meditating
- Leisure reading
- Working out
- Playing sports
- Playing with your pet
- Hanging out with friends
- Solving puzzles

---

following apps: Todoist, Upnote, Quicken Simplifi, Instapaper, Lichess, and Google Suite. Thus, I have six if I count the Google Suite as one app.

- People watching
- Listening to live music

Review your list of favorite activities the next time you're tempted to reach for your phone. Ask yourself, "What could I be doing instead?"

Take Breaks from Social Media and the News Cycle

We've covered several ways to reduce the digital noise in your life. Many of them will also help you scale down the time you spend on social media and news-related sites. You have the tools you need to make it happen.

But it's worth highlighting *why* you should scale down your time on these platforms. As noted above, they're designed to trigger the release of dopamine. That's reason enough to avoid them. But there are additional reasons.

Social media inflames a fear of missing out. You can't help but notice how others *seem* to be living a better, funner, and more rewarding life than you.* You end up feeling inferior and insecure. You start to feel anxious that you're out of the loop and being left behind. These feelings are not conducive to embracing a slower-paced life.

News-related sites present a different problem. They prioritize doom and gloom. These sites place bad news front and center because their algorithms show that such news drives more engagement (views, clicks, shares, etc.).

---

* More often than not, this is a carefully manufactured mirage.

But bad news also provokes and inflames feelings of anxiety. This is called headline stress disorder. This anxiety is indefensible if you hope to embrace a slower, more mindful, more *meaningful* lifestyle.

For these reasons, you must take regular breaks from social media and the 24-hour news cycle. The longer your breaks, the better. Neither social media nor nonstop doom and gloom will improve your quality of life. Indeed, both are likely to undermine it.

As with weaning yourself from your phone, take small steps to wean yourself from these platforms. Start with 60-minute breaks. Then, try to avoid these platforms for two hours. Then, try four hours. You'll eventually find that avoiding them for weeks makes you feel more optimistic, calm, and energetic.

∿

EXERCISE #7

∿

THE PURPOSE of this exercise is to identify the triggers that compel you to seek digital recreation. Once you're aware of the triggers, you can take action toward countering them.

Whenever you reach for your phone, tablet, or any other device, ask yourself what provokes the urge. Do you feel stressed and believe your phone will serve as a salve?

Are you bored and crave entertainment? Do you fear that you're missing out on something important?

Do the same whenever you feel compelled to check social media. Do you feel lonely and desire social interaction? Are you struggling with a poor self-image and long for external validation? Has something angered you to the point that you need to express your opinion?

Now, do likewise whenever you feel the urge to read your news feed. Do you want to keep up with current events to avoid feeling left out among your friends? Do you feel social pressure to stay informed and conversant about geopolitics? Do you want to be considered an expert on recent happenings? If so, is this desire incited by low self-esteem?

Time required: 20 minutes

STEP 8: PRACTICE INTENTIONAL COMMUNICATION

> The single biggest problem in communication is the illusion that it has taken place.
>
> — GEORGE BERNARD SHAW

The way we communicate says a lot about our frame of mind. You know this from experience. You've been on the receiving end of it. You've spoken with people so distracted they're hardly hearing you. They constantly break eye contact as their attention is seized by activity in your immediate surroundings. Or their eyes gloss over as their thoughts wander to things unrelated to your conversation.

Perhaps you do this to others. Do you struggle to be fully present when you talk or listen to people? During conversations, are you constantly distracted by your environment, internal chatter, or wandering thoughts?

If so, this may be due to mental turbulence caused by an always-on-the-go lifestyle. When you're accustomed to rushing around, it isn't easy to be fully present in the here and now. It's hard to slow down and focus on the other person. The mental pandemonium from nonstop hustling consumes your attention.

You can counter this cognitive chaos by sharpening your communication skills. Doing so will train your mind to slow down and be present. You'll communicate intentionally rather than just going through the motions, pretending to listen, and speaking without purpose. You'll learn to control the spontaneous thoughts running through your head that drain your ability to focus.

Improve Your Face-to-Face Communication Skills

Face-to-face communication is about more than just conveying information, ideas, and opinions and allowing the other person to do the same. It's mainly about *how* you do so and *what* you do while the other person does it.

If you're constantly in a rush, you'll be less mindful during conversations. You'll be more easily distracted. You may be overly verbose, unaware you're using 1,000 words when 100 would suffice. You might even repeat details unnecessarily.

Or you might be inclined to approach the conversation like other tasks: you want to get it done quickly because you have a million other things to do. Consequently, you might feel compelled to interrupt the other person, talk over them, or wait impatiently as they speak. You may also miss critical non-verbal cues like facial expressions, hand gestures, and body language.

Improving your face-to-face communication skills encourages you to slow down. It urges you to let go of the impulse to worry about "what's next" and instead be present during conversations. Instead of representing to-do items, your conversations become opportunities to engage authentically with others.

It takes time to develop and sharpen these skills. Here are three simple tips you can put to use immediately:

1. **Work on being concise**. Think about what you'd like to say and use fewer words to say it. Refrain from using filler words and hedge language (for example, "I just wanted to speak with you for a second and see if you have a chance to talk about XYZ."). Be mindful regarding how you frame your message. Use simple words. Be brief. Be clear.

2. **Practice active listening**. Give your full attention to the speaker. Don't judge what they're saying. Don't form responses or rebuttals while they're talking. Just listen. Focus on the speaker's message and their purpose for sharing it. When they've finished speaking, reflect on what they said. Summarize it to

ensure you understand it. If necessary, ask for clarification.

3. **Watch for visual cues**. Pay attention to the other person's body language and facial expressions. Are they furrowing their brow or crossing their arms while you speak? Are they shaking their head in disagreement? Or are they doing so in a show of commiseration? Do they appear nervous? Distracted? Perturbed? Are they mirroring your body language and facial expressions, both of which suggest they're listening attentively to you?

You'll find that improving your face-to-face communication skills has a cyclic effect. As noted earlier, doing so encourages you to adopt a slower pace. This, in turn, enables you to hone your communication skills further. As they grow, these skills will help you avoid unnecessary conflict, develop empathy and compassion, and enhance the quality of your most important relationships.

Improve Your Written Communication Skills

Sharing information, ideas, and opinions in written form is arguably more difficult than in person. You don't benefit from non-verbal cues like facial expressions and hand gestures. You can't tell whether the reader is engaged or disinterested. There's no way for you to know whether they agree with you or strongly oppose what you're telling them (at least until they respond, which might take days or weeks). All you have are the words you choose and how you present them.

It's tempting to write quickly and presume your message will have the effect you want. However, as with face-to-face communication, how you communicate in written form determines how your message comes across— if it gets across at all.

If you use too many words, the recipient will start skimming or stop reading entirely. If you use too few words, the recipient will be confused and irritated. If you fail to organize your thoughts, the reader will struggle to see your point. If you fail to edit, you might inadvertently convey the wrong ideas.

These communication habits are most likely to surface when you're in a hurry. Distracted by other tasks, commitments, and assorted mental preoccupations, these habits undermine your emails and texts; they weaken your memos, letters, and proposals; they compromise your reports and presentations.

Curbing these bad habits and honing your written communication skills forces you to slow down and think carefully about what you're writing. It urges you to temporarily set aside the tasks, commitments, and mental preoccupations competing for your time and attention. In doing so, you train yourself to write mindfully. To choose your words carefully. To write to get your point across as effectively as possible.

As with face-to-face communication, building and

refining these skills takes time. But you can do so easily with a bit of practice. Here are three quick tips that will help:

1. **Strip it down**. The simpler you write, the more precise your message. Ironically, writing simply requires a fair bit of thought and effort. It's easy to fill space with useless jargon and fancy phrasing. It's much harder to strip down your writing to the bare essentials.

2. **Be specific**. The biggest roadblock to clarity is vagueness. Specificity removes this roadblock. The people who read your emails, texts, memos, and letters should never struggle to figure out what you're saying. They should get your point immediately. The best way to ensure they do is to use precise language.

3. **Note your tone**. The tone of your writing is crucial because you can't rely on non-verbal cues. Think about your purpose, circumstances, and the reader's expectations. Are you responding to a heartfelt letter from a friend who's feeling vulnerable? Or are you writing an email to the CEO of your company? Slow down and reflect on whether you want your message to be compassionate and uplifting or diplomatic and informative.

Effective writing requires thoughtfulness. That's the

main reason for improving this skill (as it relates to the aim of this book). Thoughtful writing necessitates slowing down to choose the right words and most appropriate phrasing. It calls for pausing the busyness of your day to ensure you get your message across as clearly as possible.

Look Through the Other Person's Lens

To communicate effectively with your audience, you must see the world through their eyes. This will allow you to tailor your message to convey the necessary details and produce the desired effect.

This requires thoughtfulness and reflection, as well as active listening and reading. It also entails observing the other person's nonverbal cues, tone, and phrasing, asking clarifying questions, and filling in gaps when the other person refuses to be explicit.

To do this successfully, you need to take a breather from the whirlwind of your day. You won't be able to see things from your audience's perspective if you're in a rush and your mind is consumed by other thoughts and tasks. So, take a break from the chaos, find a few moments of calm, and ask yourself the following questions about the other person:

- What information do they already possess?
- What additional information do they need?
- What biases do they have?
- What assumptions are they making?

- What judgments have they formed?
- What emotions are they feeling?
- What stressors are they experiencing?
- What roadblocks are they encountering?

Asking these questions puts you in their shoes. It helps you to relate to their viewpoint. Answering these questions (at least, to the best of your ability) allows you to bridge gaps that would otherwise muddy your message, distort it, or sabotage it entirely.

Enough theory. Let's do an exercise to apply these tips and ideas.

EXERCISE #8

THIS EXERCISE IS a post-conversation audit.* It involves asking yourself focused questions that help you evaluate your communication. It will also reveal areas for improvement.

---

* We'll focus on face-to-face communication because it involves many elements we can monitor and refine. It also provides near-immediate feedback. I encourage you to use a similar process to audit your written communication. However, note that it may take much longer to receive actionable feedback.

After each conversation or presentation, ask yourself the following questions:

- Was I clear? Or was I nebulous?
- Was I concise? Or was I verbose?
- Was I precise? Or was I vague?
- Did I use simple words? Or did I use complex jargon, archaic terms, and flowery language?
- Did my tone and delivery match my intention?
- Was I mindful of the other person's non-verbal cues?
- Did they seem confused by what I said? Angered? Dismissive?
- Did I give them my full attention while they talked? Did I listen actively to what they said?
- Did I understand their perspective and empathize with their feelings and frame of mind?

These questions allow you to scrutinize specific aspects of your communication to improve them. They allow you to identify and develop skills you lack or polish those that have become dull and rusty.

Time required: 10 minutes

STEP 9: CULTIVATE AN ATTITUDE OF GRATITUDE

66 We spend precious hours fearing the inevitable. It would be wise to use that time adoring our families, cherishing our surroundings, and embracing our gifts.

— MAYA ANGELOU

Practicing gratitude can feel unnatural, especially if you maintain a frantic pace. It is the antithesis of hustle culture, a counterpoint to today's rise-and-grind ethos. It contradicts the clamor and pandemonium of today's "get more done" climate.

The problem is that if you're like most people, you spend most of your time, energy, and attention on the chaos of constant busyness. That leaves few resources available to sustain a grateful mindset.

That alone is reason enough to reflect on why it's important to practice gratitude. The fact that speeding through life is preventing you from recognizing the positives should be an eye-opener.

Cultivating an appreciative attitude requires slowing down to reflect and celebrate. It calls for taking a break from the nonstop rushing and contemplating all you have to be thankful for.

Doing so doesn't come easy. It might feel awkward or unsettling if you've never done it. Below, I'll show you how to counter this resistance and slowly develop a gratitude habit.

It'll be time well invested. Once you adopt this practice, you'll feel less anxious and stressed. You'll feel happier and more content. You'll sleep better. You'll have greater control over toxic emotions. You'll have more patience and resilience when you face life's myriad inconveniences and frustrations.

In short, you have a lot to gain by regularly practicing gratitude. It can literally improve your quality of life.

Keep a Daily Gratitude Journal

Journaling about the things you're thankful for has two benefits. First, it offers a dedicated place to return to each day to express your gratitude privately. Your journal becomes a repository of your appreciative thoughts. You'll regularly add to it and revisit it whenever you feel dispirited to remind yourself of all you have to be grateful for.

The second benefit of keeping a daily gratitude journal is that it helps you to adopt a life-changing habit. When you acknowledge the positives in your life each day, doing so becomes part of your routine. The more you do it, the more ingrained it becomes and the more natural it feels. Over time, you'll look forward to doing it because it brings you joy and solace. It offers a respite from the stress and anxiety of your day.

Keeping a gratitude journal is simple and easy. But there are a few best practices that will help you make the most of this discipline.

1. **Be precise**. Rather than writing, "I'm grateful for my family," be specific. Which family member do you feel appreciation for? Was there a particular incident that evoked this feeling? The more precise you are, the more connected you'll feel to whatever inspired your gratitude.

2. **Let go of entitlement**. If you feel entitled to the good things you have or experience, you won't fully appreciate them. You'll take them for granted. Treat them as lucky circumstances. When you note them in your journal, consider your good fortune.

3. **Focus on people**. It's easier to connect with relationships than with circumstances and possessions. While expressing gratitude for your

job, home, and lottery winnings is fine, it's your relationships that will bring enduring joy and fulfillment.

4. **Keep it simple**. You'll enjoy this practice more if you write simply. You'll find it easier to express your thoughts when you're not burdened by an impulse to use big words or pretentious phrasing. Also, don't feel obligated to write a paragraph when a few words suffice. That adds unnecessary pressure.

5. **Use prompts**. It's hard to write on a blank page. Prompts give you a jumping-off point. They help you to focus on something specific. They'll also encourage honesty and openness and trigger your creativity.

10 Quickstart Gratitude Journaling Prompts

The following prompts are merely ideas. Use them as inspiration to develop your prompts.

1. What is one trait I admire in {insert name}?
2. What is one thing I regularly take for granted?
3. What is one aspect of my neighborhood that I enjoy?
4. What is one feature of my job that I like?
5. Who has always been emotionally supportive of me? How have they shown their support?

6. What is one thing I did today that brought me joy or made me feel calm?
7. What is one skill I possess that has improved my quality of life?
8. What is my favorite time of day? Why?
9. What always makes me smile (e.g., puns, pet videos, baby's laughter, etc.)?
10. What recently made me feel good physically (e.g., a warm beverage, a favorite food, a leisurely walk, etc.)?

Keeping a daily gratitude journal can soothe an otherwise stressful, frustrating day. Most importantly, it encourages you to slow down and savor your relationships, experiences, and other positives you might otherwise overlook.

Take a Daily Gratitude Walk

This is one of the simplest activities you can do, and it's always rewarding. You go on a walk and acknowledge things you're grateful for.

As with writing in your gratitude journal, these walks are an opportunity to disengage from the busyness of your day. To enjoy a break from the rush and commotion of your schedule, duties, and commitments. They are a chance to bask in the present rather than worry about what's around the corner.

As you walk, recognize the things you value in your life.

Celebrate your friends and loved ones. Observe recent experiences that made you smile, laugh, or feel joyful. Acknowledge your access to food, shelter, and other necessities. Consider your material possessions that improve your quality of life (e.g., your home, vehicle, computer, etc.).

Carry an index card or small sheet of paper that lists your favorite gratitude journaling prompts. A quick look at these prompts will help sharpen your focus and get the ball rolling.

The best part of this activity is that you control how your walks unfold. If you only have five minutes, go on a 5-minute walk. If you have a clear schedule, take a 60-minute walk. Do you live near a park or hiking trail? If so, enjoy the peace and calm of walking in nature. Is the weather terrible? If so, walk indoors. There's no right or wrong way to do this.

I recommend walking alone. The solitude will help you focus on what you're grateful for. You might also enjoy a gratitude walk with a trusted friend or family member. Take turns expressing your appreciation for the people, experiences, and other positives you value. As a bonus, this time together will reinforce the emotional connection and intimacy you share with this person.

Identify Circumstances You're Taking for Granted

It's natural to take things for granted. All of us do it, usually without realizing it. We overlook things we should appreciate. We neglect the positive aspects of our lives, focusing instead on the trivial inconveniences we encounter each day. And even when we acknowledge the advantages we enjoy and the assets we possess, we often undervalue them. We underestimate their significance.

This happens for many reasons. Sometimes, we're consumed by the chaos of our day and thus overlook the blessings we should treasure. Sometimes, we grow so accustomed to how things are that we assume they'll always be so. Sometimes, we take things for granted because they become a part of our routine. Constant exposure dulls their value in our eyes. An example of this is lottery winners, for whom the novelty of winning the lottery eventually wears off.*

To cultivate an attitude of gratitude, we need to resist this tendency. We need to counter our brain's penchant for habituation. Here are three practical, actionable tips that will help you do so:

1. **Do without**. Choose something you enjoy
   (e.g., your favorite wine, a particular venue, your
   gaming console, etc.) and temporarily abstain
   from it. Depending on how often you typically
   indulge, this could mean a couple of days or
   several weeks. When you come back to it, you'll
   appreciate it more.

---

* The fancy term for this phenomenon is hedonic adaptation. Humans return to a baseline of happiness following significant events, whether positive or negative.

2. **Seek new experiences**. Learn a new skill. Try a new activity. Take a new route home from your job. Buy groceries at a store you've never visited. This will challenge your brain's tendency to grow accustomed to how things are.

3. **Upend your routines**. Do you visit the same coffeeshop on your way to your job each morning? Visit a different one or make coffee (or tea) at home. Do you usually end your day by streaming your favorite shows? Read a book or do a crossword puzzle instead. Do you typically scroll through social media while eating lunch? Listen to a podcast as an alternative.

You'll notice a gradual change in your outlook as you actively acknowledge the relationships, possessions, advantages, and blessings you usually take for granted. The positive aspects of your life will appear more prominently. The silver linings of your life will shine more brightly. You'll find yourself more inclined to embrace and savor the present instead of perpetually chasing the next thing.

～

EXERCISE #9

～

GRAB a pen and sheet of paper, and find a quiet place free of distractions. Write a short letter to a cherished friend or loved one. Ideally, this will be an individual to whom you've never expressed your appreciation for their being a part of your life.

Before we get into the details of what your letter should include, note that you won't need to present this letter to your friend or loved one. You can keep it private if you prefer. It can be for your eyes only.

The value of this exercise is in *writing* the letter. Documenting your thoughts will force your brain to recognize this individual's positive impact on you. It will bring into sharper focus how they improve your quality of life.

Don't worry about the words you choose as you write your letter. Don't stress over whether your letter is structured well. Don't get hung up on whether it even makes sense.

Simply write to your friend or loved one.

What should you write? Here are a few questions to ask yourself as prompts:

- What are three things I love about them?
- What do I miss when they're not around?
- What is a memorable experience we shared?
- What was a meaningful conversation we had?
- What would my life be like if they weren't in it?
- How have they helped me in the past?
- What reminds me of them?
- What preferences and pet peeves do we share?

- How did we meet?

As you write your letter, pay close attention to how you feel. What emotions are you experiencing? What images are appearing in your head? What memories are coming to mind?

The last time I did this exercise, I became teary-eyed. It revealed to me what I had been taking for granted.

Don't be surprised if you have a similar experience. Embrace it. Savor it. Let the moment engulf you. Use it to fuel your blossoming attitude of gratitude.

Time required: 20 minutes

STEP 10: PERFORM A WEEKLY REVIEW

> The only real mistake is the one from which we learn nothing.
>
> — HENRY FORD

I t isn't easy to know how much progress you've made unless you reflect on the recent past. That's the purpose of doing a weekly review. It allows you to wrap up the week by taking stock of what transpired and using that information to plan for the following week.

This is your chance to evaluate your decisions and actions and appraise their individual and cumulative effect on your goal to live a slower-paced life. It's your chance to measure your progress and ensure you're on the right track. During your weekly review, you'll answer questions such as the following:

- Did my decisions and actions over the past week align with my intention?
- Did they produce the results I expected?
- What successes did I experience?
- What mistakes did I make?
- What lessons did I learn about myself?
- What challenges or roadblocks did I encounter?
- What solutions or workarounds did I implement? Were they effective?
- How does the past week compare to the one before it?

Your weekly review will give you clarity. It will reveal what worked and what didn't. These details will inform your future decisions and actions, giving you increasingly more control over your results.

Before we begin, pick a day of the week on which you have 30 minutes to perform this activity undisturbed. I review my week on Sundays because my mind thinks of Sunday as the end of the week. But choose the day that works best for you.

With that sorted, let's jump in.

Record Your Hits and Misses

Weekly reviews are traditionally performed to track productivity and task management. During these reviews, you would evaluate your progress on the goals, tasks, and projects you worked on the previous week.

Here, we're taking a more holistic approach. Naturally, you had goals you wanted to achieve related to adopting a slower, more mindful pace (e.g., saying "no" more often and letting go of optional commitments). You had tasks you wanted to complete (e.g., organizing your digital life and practicing active listening). You had projects you wanted to advance (e.g., gradually incorporating the ten activities in Step 6 to help reshape your mindset) into your day.

But we're not exclusively concerned with whether you completed everything. That's not the top priority. Instead, our focus is on what worked and what didn't in the context of learning to embrace a slow-living ethos.

Review your actions over the past week pertaining to this goal. For each of them, ask yourself the following questions:

- What went well?
- What went poorly?
- Where did I struggle?
- What should I do differently?
- What did I learn about myself?

For example, suppose last week you worked on your willingness and ability to say no to people. You tried a variety of tactics across a range of scenarios. Ask yourself the following questions:

- Was I able to successfully decline requests and invitations?
- Was I able to maintain my boundaries?
- Did I capitulate in the end? If yes, what was the tipping point?
- Did I feel guilty for saying no? If yes, what triggered this feeling?
- What different tactics can I try next week?
- What lessons can I take away from the experience?

Every action goes under the microscope during your weekly review. The purpose isn't to beat yourself up for poor results. There's no value in that. Instead, the purpose is to assess what worked and what didn't. If you keep doing the former and pivot on the latter, you'll enjoy more wins and face fewer struggles in the coming weeks.

Refine Your Habits and Routines

Recording your hits and misses hinges on reflection. It's now time to act on the insights you've gained. We'll focus on your habits and routines, reinforcing the ones that support a slower-paced lifestyle and changing those that undermine it.

Let's return to our example of saying no to people. Suppose after a couple of weekly reviews, the following behavioral patterns become apparent:

- When a neighbor asks you for a favor, you immediately commit.
- When a friend asks for money, you reflexively reach for your wallet or purse.
- When an acquaintance invites you to a social event, you automatically accept their invitation.
- When a coworker asks you to attend a meeting, you impulsively add it to your calendar.

These automatic responses compromise your intention to slow down. So, you must figure out what prompts them. Habits have triggers. They have psychological cues. Once you have identified them, you can disrupt them. Then you replace them.

For example, suppose you've discovered that you usually say yes to people for the following reasons:

- You assume you're obligated.
- You hope to be liked.
- You want to avoid being judged.
- You believe you should cede to authority.
- You feel compelled to reciprocate.
- You try to model others' behaviors.

- You think you'll miss an opportunity.

Now that you've identified these cues, you can make plans to interrupt or circumvent them. For example, you can try the following:

- Challenge the sense of obligation you're feeling.
- Remind yourself that not everyone will like you.
- Accept that others will judge you.
- Question your instinct to submit to authority.
- Consider whether reciprocity is required.
- Disregard your impulse to model other people.
- Ask yourself whether you'll truly miss out on an opportunity you want.

These actions will gradually help you to break the habit of saying yes. And importantly, they'll help you to replace that habit with a healthier one: recognizing that saying no is always an option.

The broader scope of this discussion is that this process is an integral part of your weekly reviews. This practice may seem daunting and overwhelming, but that feeling may stem from our example in this section.*

Once you've incorporated weekly reviews into your

---

* I used this example because saying no will have a profound, far-reaching, and enduring impact on your goal to embrace a slower-paced lifestyle.

routine, you'll find they're simple and easy to do. You may even find them fun.

Recognize and Celebrate Your Progress

This section is a quick reminder of something you know intuitively. You also know it from personal experience.

A large part of embracing an unhurried, more mindful, and intentional life revolves around changing your frame of mind. But doing so can be complicated. You'll be unraveling years of conditioning.

One of the most effective tools you can use to this end is also one of the simplest: noting your progress and giving yourself credit for it. When you acknowledge the positive changes you've made and the milestones you've reached, you feel *good* about yourself. You have an opportunity to revel in your achievement.

Your brain releases dopamine, which triggers these feelings. These feelings reinforce your actions and your adopted healthy habits and routines.

Make this a part of your weekly review. Recognize your progress during the previous week, even if you experienced some setbacks. *Especially* if you experienced some setbacks. Acknowledge that progress. Celebrate your wins. Take pride in them.

If you've never done this, you'll be astonished at how powerful it is as a motivator to keep moving forward.

~

EXERCISE #10

IN THIS FINAL EXERCISE, we'll create a simple template you can use for your weekly reviews. You don't want to start from scratch each time you sit down to review your week. That would waste valuable time. This template will allow you to spend that time *reviewing*.

I recommend doing this digitally, ideally in a spreadsheet. That way, you can easily add, delete, and move things around as you see fit.

Create the following three sections:

1. Actions to Review
2. Questions to Ask
3. Strategies to Try

The first section can be left blank. But give yourself enough room to document three actions to scrutinize. Three is the maximum. By limiting your weekly reviews to three items, you can give each one the time and attention it deserves.

Under the second section, write the following five questions:

1. What went well?
2. What went poorly?
3. Where did I struggle?

4. What should I do differently?

5. What did I learn about myself?

You'll ask these questions for each of the three actions you've noted in the first section.

The third section can be left blank, similar to the first section. But again, give yourself room to make notes. Here is where you'll brainstorm tactics to try during the following week. Again, three is the maximum. Don't overdo it by listing 20 things to try.

You now have a simple template you can use each week, which will save you time and help you be consistent. But it's just a starting point. I encourage you to tailor it to suit your goals and circumstances.

When you review the previous week, open your template and rename it using the "Save As" feature. I recommend using the following naming convention:

Week ending XXXX/YY/ZZ

XXXX is the year. YY is the day. ZZ is the month. This file naming system will allow you to quickly sort your reviews by date and revisit select weeks whenever you desire.*

---

* If you prefer, you can use analog tools like paper and pen. However, doing so will make organizing your weekly reviews and revisiting select weeks more difficult.

Time required: 15 minutes

PART III

HOW TO EMBRACE THE ART OF GOING SLOW ACROSS YOUR LIFE

∼

You've just completed the most challenging part of this book. You've mastered the steps to adopt a slower-paced lifestyle that will improve your quality of life.

But how do you apply what you've learned to your everyday experience? Where can you implement the ideas and advice you've read so you'll reap the biggest benefits?

In this section, we'll explore major life categories and discuss how and where you can apply the knowledge and insights you've acquired. It's chock full of tips and strategies you can use *today*. But note that what follows is merely a springboard. The purpose of this section is to inspire your own ideas. After all, you're the captain of your ship. You get to shape your life in the manner you desire.

YOUR CAREER

Don't let making a living prevent you from making a life.

— JOHN WOODEN

I f you work full-time, your job is a significant part of your life. Whether you're a freelancer working from home, a contractor working remotely, or a business professional with a corner office, your career is a big part of your day-to-day.

You take pride in your career and strive to do well. You hope to get ahead, earn recognition, build your reputation, and receive pay raises for your hard work.

It's easy to become consumed by these desires. The downside is that it opens the door for your job to bleed into your personal life. Working an occasional evening or weekend is unavoidable. But it's a slippery slope. If you don't install safeguards, you might regularly sacrifice your downtime for career growth.

So, let's talk about a few protective measures you can implement to prevent this from happening.

Set Professional Boundaries

This is a delicate operation. You need to define and communicate what you consider acceptable and unacceptable among your colleagues. But you'll want to do so in a way that avoids unnecessary conflict. It's a balancing act. One that requires resolve and tact.

You'll want to set professional boundaries to preserve your mental well-being, stay productive, and maintain a healthy work-life balance. For example:

- Avoid office gossip and useless arguments. Both waste time, erode trust, cause divisiveness, and hurt morale.
- Be willing to say "no" more often. Turn down projects that aren't your responsibility. Decline meetings for which your participation is unnecessary.
- Limit the amount of overtime you put in. Taking work home or working late hours is fine on occasion. But if you do so regularly, ask yourself whether your workload is reasonable.

- Resist the urge to read and respond to non-urgent work texts you receive late at night. Most of them can wait until the following morning.
- When you're trying to focus, reject unnecessary interruptions. Ask the individual if you can follow up with them when you're available.
- Respect your coworkers' boundaries. It's difficult to enforce your own if you're dismissive and cavalier toward theirs.

Communicate your professional boundaries. Don't expect others to recognize them on their own. Be prepared to express some of your expectations directly to select individuals. For example, if a colleague repeatedly interrupts you, tell them you need to work without distraction.

You'll be able to convey other boundaries with the tools you use each day, such as your daily calendar.

Time Block Your Calendar

Time blocking means allocating every moment of your day. Your day is organized into blocks of time, and each block is assigned a particular purpose. This might sound complicated, but it's actually simple. It's also beneficial in several important ways:

- It identifies what you should do and when you should do it, with zero ambiguity.

- It allows you to set the pace of your day. You determine in advance what you'll do and when you'll do it.
- It helps you to monitor your progress. Are you completing the tasks you intended to complete?
- It gives you a legitimate reason to say no to others.
- It encourages you to schedule time for rest and leisure. Neither is relegated to the back burner — or worse, disregarded entirely.
- It makes clear where and how you spend your time. You can simply review your daily calendar.
- It allows you to focus since you'll work on a singular task, activity, or project during each time block.
- It discourages procrastination. Time blocks urge you to take purposeful action at specific times of the day.
- It deters perfectionism. Time blocks limit your time to complete tasks or advance projects to a chosen milestone.

The biggest advantage of time blocking your day is that it gives you control over how your day progresses. You set the cadence. You set the tempo. You may lack *complete* control due to your responsibilities and unavoidable commitments. But time blocking grants you *more* control than you would otherwise experience.

Take Time Off

A friend once said, "Getting to the top is simple. All you have to do is sacrifice every other aspect of your life."

You probably know someone who pours everything into their job. They respond to every pressing matter, even if they're on vacation. They take work-related calls at all hours, dropping everything to intervene. For them, time off is a non-factor because they're always "on."

The irony is that this practice increases stress and anxiety, provokes mental health issues, and leads to burnout. In other words, it's likely to harm their career in the long run.

Taking time off counters these effects:

- It gives you a chance to recover from intense work and high-demand periods, allowing you to decompress.
- It allows you time to spend with loved ones, improving your mental and emotional well-being.
- It helps you stave off burnout by temporarily shielding you from your job's chaos and high pressure.

There are many other advantages you'll experience when you regularly take time off:

- **Increased creativity** - You're more likely to

come up with inspired ideas when you feel refreshed.

- **Increased productivity** - You can process information more effectively when you're relaxed.
- **Improved focus** - You can concentrate better when you're less stressed.
- **Better sleep quality** - You have more time to sleep and enjoy a greater sense of calm.
- **Work-life balance** - You have more time to spend with your family and friends and pursue hobbies that interest you.

Taking time off from your job is a bulwark against a whirlwind pace. It "forces" you to hit pause on the relentless rush and busyness that arise from career tunnel vision. It urges you to take a breather. To enjoy a much-needed, periodic hiatus from a work schedule that would otherwise threaten to overwhelm you.

YOUR INTERPERSONAL INTERACTIONS

" Too often we underestimate the power of a touch, a smile, a kind word, a listening ear, an honest compliment, or the smallest act of caring, all of which have the potential to turn a life around.

— LEO BUSCAGLIA

Taking others for granted is too easy, especially when we rush through life. We don't do it on purpose. Moreover, we know intuitively that it's inconsiderate and disrespectful. But we regularly do it, often without realizing it.

There are many reasons. We fall into routines that influence our expectations. We grow accustomed to others' willingness to help and support us and expect them to continue doing so. Sometimes, we undervalue others due to overt egoism; we feel entitled to what they can offer us.

Even when we don't take others for granted, we often fail to delight in our interactions with them. It's understandable, even if it's detrimental to our emotional wellbeing. We're busy. We're stressed. We're exhausted from our rise-and-grind lifestyle. So we're cranky with those around us. We're curt with them. We're impatient and dismissive.

This behavior leads to loneliness as our relationships deteriorate. As people begin to avoid us, we feel empty and disconnected. Social situations eventually become a chore we dread rather than a joy we look forward to.

You may have experienced this yourself. You might be experiencing it at this moment. The good news is that you can make simple changes that transform your interactions with others. You can break old patterns and implement new ones. As these new patterns take hold, you'll find that you increasingly appreciate others' humanity and individuality.

Embrace Others' Imperfections

We are all flawed. We all have shortcomings and weaknesses. We are imperfect beings who regularly make poor decisions and exhibit annoying, counterproductive, and self-defeating behaviors. We try to improve ourselves, but it's a long process, and we're not always successful.

In the interim, we want to be accepted by others. We want to be liked and trusted by them. We want to be understood, appreciated, and respected by them. This requires that they look past our flaws. It requires that they embrace our humanity and individuality by embracing our imperfections.

It's important to recognize this dynamic because connecting with other people requires the same response from us. Before we can form meaningful relationships with others, we must accept them, flaws and all. This reciprocity is the core of social chemistry and is a prerequisite for building fulfilling connections.

It's difficult to do this when we're speeding through life, constantly distracted and habitually busy. When we slow down, we give ourselves the breathing room to adjust our focus. We allow ourselves to reflect on our social habits, set aside our biases and prejudices, and learn to welcome the uniqueness we see in others.

A curious thing happens as we go through this process: we develop more compassion for our *own* imperfections. As our self-compassion grows, we become less self-conscious and more confident when interacting with others. We feel more comfortable expressing ourselves. We feel more at ease being genuine and authentic. These feelings are the catalyst that allows enriching relationships to blossom and flourish.

See Others as Real People

A hustle-and-grind attitude tends to make us view others in terms of how their actions and decisions affect us. We become solipsistic in our constant rushing. We see these individuals as resources if their actions and decisions help us. If they hinder us, even if they do so unintentionally or unknowingly, we see them as obstacles.

Instead of viewing acquaintances, friends, and even loved ones as real people, we view them as tools that serve a specific purpose. They either fulfill our needs or stand in our way.*

This mindset is counterproductive to finding joy in our interpersonal interactions. It harms our desire to form and experience gratifying, supportive, and affirming relationships.

Fortunately, you can break this mindset with a few simple practices. It'll take time, but it *will* happen if you regularly do the following three things when you speak with others:

1. **Ask curiosity questions**. Go beyond the surface-level questions (e.g., "How's it going?"). Go deeper than the ice-breakers (e.g., "What are you from?"). For example, you might ask

---

* I'm ashamed to admit that I speak from experience. I held this attitude as a young man, and my dismissive demeanor hurt people close to me. I still wince when I think about it decades later.

someone, "What are your thoughts on this topic?" Or once you've learned what they do for a living, you might ask, "What's the most challenging or frustrating part of your job?"

2. **Be an attentive listener**. Don't interrupt them. Don't think about what you'll say when they stop talking. Just listen to what they're telling you. What are they implying rather than saying explicitly? What does their body language suggest? Bonus points for maintaining eye contact (but don't make it weird by staring into their soul).

3. **Share something personal**. Personal stories reinforce our individuality and add nuance and flavor to our conversations. When you share things you've experienced, you become interesting to others. Your anecdotes grab their attention and encourage them to share their stories with you. You'll learn what makes them who they are, including their ambitions, hopes, and fears. You'll also develop empathy for them, seeing the world through their eyes.

These three practices do more than present you as pleasant, personable, and relatable. They gradually change how you perceive others. You'll begin to appreciate them as real, genuine people with all the quirks, habits, and eccentricities that make them intriguing.

YOUR LEARNING STRATEGY

 He who learns but does not think is lost. He who thinks but does not learn is in great danger.

— CONFUCIUS

I n the same way we rush through life, we tend to speed through our education. This is the case whether we're learning new skills, acquiring new knowledge, completing some form of training, or obtaining an advanced degree. We try to expedite the process. We cut corners. We take shortcuts. We compromise thoroughness to reach the finish line as quickly as possible.

While reasons vary, most of us do it because we view the endeavor as a means to an end. We learn things, pursue training, and obtain degrees as a stepping stone to achieving something else. A promotion. A raise. A new job.

However, rushing the learning experience can lead to several problems. First, our retention suffers. We learn shallowly, never genuinely committing the training or knowledge to memory. Consequently, it's not there when we need to draw on it.

Second, cutting corners and taking shortcuts leave knowledge and skill gaps. Neither may be apparent during the education process, but it becomes evident when we discover that we lack the knowledge and skills to complete tasks and projects.

Third, we fail to develop a deep interest and curiosity about what we're learning. The learning process resembles an assembly line. We take the necessary steps and slap together the requisite parts to produce an end result but with little imagination or inspiration. This harms our resourcefulness. It hampers our ability to think creatively to resolve challenges and overcome obstacles.

So, let's slow things down. Instead of rushing the learning experience, let's ease up on the accelerator. You'll improve your retention of the material you're learning. You'll avoid knowledge and skill gaps. You'll also foster genuine interest and curiosity, which will help you think creatively when you need to.

The first step is to streamline the learning process by scrapping the nonessential stuff.

Avoid Information Overload

When you're learning something new, whether to deepen your knowledge base or widen your skillset, it's natural to want to soak up as much information as possible. Every resource seems useful. Every detail appears valuable. Every insight feels worthy of attention.

The problem is that the sheer volume of information at your fingertips can quickly become overwhelming. There is no end to it online. You can technically expand your knowledge about a topic and broaden your skill repertoire forever.

If you enjoy learning, this might seem beneficial. Rewarding, even. But in reality, it imposes significant consequences. At some point, you'll eventually overload your working memory. This, in turn, will harm your productivity, impair your decision-making, and make you susceptible to "analysis paralysis." It may even lead to sleep issues, memory loss, and (ironically) an inability to process new information efficiently.

So, it's worth putting a few safeguards in place. Here are four simple tips that will help you to avoid information overload whenever you're learning something new:

1. Remind yourself that you don't need to know everything about the topic you're focused on. It's impossible to *learn* everything about the subject. So, trying to do so is a waste of time, energy, and attention.

2. Limit your resources. You don't have to read every book on the subject. You don't have to review every scientific study. You don't have to peruse every article. Focus on a few credible, pertinent inputs. Ignore the rest.

3. Use active learning strategies. Summarize what you read. Test yourself by recalling details about the material.* Practice explaining the subject to an imaginary audience, such as a group of your peers.

4. Take breaks. This is dull advice, but there's a reason it's always given. Your brain needs to recharge to remain efficient at processing new information. So, schedule short time chunks to focus on what you're learning. Take breaks between them.

These tips will slow your learning process but optimize how you use your cognitive resources. They'll focus your attention on what's relevant and help you to engage with the subject you're learning.

Extend Your Timeframe

In college, a friend and I decided to take a semester off and travel through Europe. In those days, you were expected to earn your undergraduate degree within four

---

* This is known as retrieval practice.

years. If you took longer, you were doing it wrong. And sure enough, our friends and loved ones acted like we were committing a cardinal sin.

Taking a semester off had zero impact on our careers. We received our respective degrees a few months after we otherwise would have, and life went on. I'm glad we made that decision. We created memories I'll treasure for the rest of my life.

I mention this episode because there's so much pressure to speed-run your learning experience. Pressure from others. Pressure from yourself. Pressure from expectations that arise from cultural norms. Learning slowly is looked upon with disdain. It's met with subtle (and sometimes not so subtle) disapproval because it subverts expectations.

But there are notable advantages to extending your timeframe and slowing your pace:

- You have more time to absorb and reflect on what you're learning.
- You have more freedom to explore subjects that intrigue you.
- You have more latitude in thinking creatively about how to apply the material to your day-to-day life.
- You maintain a healthier balance between your education and your professional, home, social, and spiritual life.
- You retain the material longer because you're

thinking creatively and critically about it and applying it to real-world situations.

- You adapt more effectively to challenges related to the material because you've mastered it rather than skimmed through it.

These advantages hold true whether you're pursuing a college degree, seeking professional certification, attending vocational training, or working through a self-paced course. So consider slowing your pace and extending your time-frame, even if doing so defies cultural norms and contradicts others' expectations.

Learn for Self-Efficacy

At its simplest, self-efficacy means believing in yourself. It means trusting that you can perform a particular task, complete a certain project, or accomplish a specific goal. It means recognizing your talents, abilities, and expertise. It means having the confidence to take purposeful action to achieve your desired results.

Self-efficacy influences every area of your life. It plays an essential role in your daily habits. It affects your resilience during difficult situations. It impacts your confidence at work and in your personal pursuits. It reverberates in every relationship you maintain.

Rather than treating learning as a means to an end, see it as a way to cultivate greater self-efficacy. Don't just hurriedly skim and memorize what you're learning. Slow down and absorb it. Engage with it. Internalize and master it. While skimming and memorizing can help you in the short term, high self-efficacy stemming from true mastery of a subject will pay dividends for the rest of your life.

YOUR HEALTH AND NUTRITION

> Take care of your body. It's the only place you
> have to live.
>
> —JIM ROHN

Among the first casualties of hustle culture is our
attention to our fitness and nutritional habits.
We make questionable dietary choices. We
spend less time exercising (if any time at all). We sacrifice
sleep to get more done.

If we allow this to continue unchecked, our physical
health starts to suffer. We gain weight. We become fatigued
more quickly than usual. We get sick more often. We begin
to experience chronic aches and pains.

We rarely notice these issues as they develop and

become problematic. We're too busy rushing around to pay heed to them. So, they eventually take us by surprise. One day, we suddenly realize how we look and feel is light-years away from our ideal.

When you abandon hustle culture and adopt a slower-paced lifestyle, you give yourself more time to prioritize and invest in your fitness and nutrition. You have more freedom to look after both. You can address them with full awareness and make deliberate, intentional choices to strive toward your ideal.

Exercise and Eat Mindfully

Your fitness and dietary habits profoundly affect how you look and feel. But recognizing this fact doesn't make it easier to approach either of them mindfully. You may need to unravel deeply rooted routines.

Perhaps you've spent years neglecting exercise and living off coffee and fast food. Maybe you joined a gym but visit sporadically. Perhaps you frequently adopt healthy nutritional habits, but they never last. The busyness of a fast-paced life intervenes and distracts you.

So, let's go through a few simple practices you can start doing today to disrupt and dismantle old patterns. These are small actions you can take immediately to start treating your fitness and diet mindfully. Let's begin with exercise:

- **Exercise for five minutes each day**. Of course, this won't give you the physique you've always wanted. The purpose is to get your mind and body accustomed to daily exercise.

- **Start with low-impact exercises**. Walking. Swimming. Cycling. Yoga. Tai chi. They're easy to do, so you'll experience less mental resistance.
- **Alternate exercises to stay engaged**. If you walk on Monday, do tai chi on Tuesday. If you swim on Wednesday, do yoga on Thursday. Mix it up to avoid boredom.
- **Exercise alone**. To be sure there are benefits to having a workout buddy. But there's also a risk of putting exercise on the back burner if your partner can't make it.
- **Be aware of how you feel while exercising**. If you're in pain, stop. If you experience shortness of breath, stop. Nausea? Stop. The goal isn't to push yourself past your limits.

Now, let's shift our focus to eating:

- **Taste what you're eating**. Savor the flavors. Enjoy the experience.
- **Eliminate digital distractions while you eat**. Turn off your television. Set aside your phone or tablet. You'll find it easier to enjoy your meals.

- **Eat slowly**. Chew more. While chewing, set your food (or utensils) aside. Focus on what you're chewing rather than the next bite.
- **Cook your meal**. This gives you time to think about what you'll be eating. When you finally sit down to enjoy what you've prepared, you'll be less inclined to inhale it.
- **Eat with others**. Indulge in lively conversation. Discuss what you're eating, including why you like it. You'll strengthen existing relationships, and you might build new ones.

Note that every practice listed above is designed to encourage a slower pace. They're intended to support a more mindful approach to your fitness and diet routines.

Enjoy Better Sleep

Sleep is a peculiar topic. Most people recognize its importance but disregard it. They acknowledge their need for quality sleep but routinely brush it aside to attend to other priorities. While doing so may be necessary occasionally, it becomes a pattern for many people. They sacrifice sleep as a recurring practice.

The price is considerable. When you regularly neglect sleep, you compromise the following:

- Physical health

- Mental health
- Emotional health
- Cognitive performance
- Energy level
- Stress level
- Resilience to adversity
- Memory
- Weight
- Ability to learn and process information
- Immunity to disease

You have a lot to lose by sacrificing your sleep. Or, to frame it more positively, you have a lot to gain by improving it and ensuring you get enough of it each night. With that in mind, here are a few simple tips you can implement tonight:

- Follow a relaxing pre-sleep routine. Take a warm shower. Read a book. Listen to a calming playlist. Write in your journal.
- Go to bed at the same time each evening. Be consistent so your body and mind get used to it. While we're on the topic, wake up at the same time each morning (even Saturdays and Sundays).
- Maintain a cool temperature in your bedroom. Aim for 66°F (or 19°C).*

---

* Cool temperatures cause the brain to release melatonin. Often called

- Limit napping. If you enjoy taking naps, keep them under 30 minutes.
- Maintain a "no screen" policy 60 minutes before going to sleep. No phone. No tablet. No laptop.*

It may take time to get used to doing the above. But if you do them each evening, you'll fall asleep more quickly and enjoy better sleep throughout the night.

Focus On Gradual, Consistent Improvement

We've covered a lot of actionable tips in this chapter. This is a good time to reiterate the merit of taking things slowly. If you fast-track these changes, they won't stick. They'll fade away, probably before they have any lasting impact on your quality of life.

So, take your time implementing them. Remember, there's no need to rush things. This is not a race to the finish line. Instead, what matters is forming good habits pertaining to your health and nutrition, ones that'll last throughout your life.

Implementing these changes gradually and methodically is the best way to ensure this happens. Focus on being consistent. Over time, slowly but surely, they'll take root,

---

the sleep hormone, melatonin helps you to fall asleep.
* Some e-readers are fine because they rely on ambient light. A few are even designed to emit less blue and more orange light as the day progresses.

become second nature to you, and start to produce noticeable dividends. Here are a few suggestions to help you get started on the right foot:

- **Make one change at a time**. Do that one thing daily for several days. Then, make another change. Do *it* for several days. Then, make another change. Repeat this process, stacking changes on top of each other.
- **Ease into it**. Some of the changes you'll be making may feel like major lifestyle adjustments. For example, even low-impact exercises can seem challenging if you're accustomed to a sedentary lifestyle. Start small. Don't walk for 60 minutes in the beginning. Walk for 10 minutes. Don't try to cook Beef Wellington if you've never prepared a meal. Cook a simple steak.
- **Forgive your missteps**. If you slip up, don't worry about it. Acknowledge it, forgive yourself, and move on. Focus on the following day. For example, if you neglect to exercise today, identify the reason (a hectic schedule, laziness, forgetfulness, etc.). Then, recommit and exercise tomorrow. You don't have to be perfect.

Be patient with yourself. You'll make mistakes. You'll experience setbacks. That's fine. It's to be expected.

Making lifestyle changes, big or small, is rarely as simple as it seems at the outset.

The important thing is that you stay consistent and be ready to bounce back when you lose your way. It's a good investment of your time, attention, and energy. You stand to reap a transformative payoff in the long run. The cumulative benefit of these and other changes on your health and nutrition — and, by extension, your quality of life — can be extraordinary.

YOUR DECISION-MAKING PROCESS

 It's better to go slow in the right direction than to go fast in the wrong direction.

— SIMON SINEK

Sometimes, we agonize over decisions. Even the small ones. We become anxious, lose confidence, and worry about the potential consequences of making bad choices.

Sometimes, we rush our decisions. We feel pressured to move forward. We want to close open loops. Or we feel overly confident, presuming a positive outcome. Or we feel compelled to conform to established norms.

Both situations can occur when your day-to-day is frantic and chaotic. You're more susceptible to distractions.

Everything seems urgent. It feels like there's no time to pause and evaluate information about the decisions you need to make.

When you embrace an unhurried lifestyle, you give yourself the latitude to work through the decision-making process at a sensible pace. You're less likely to agonize over decisions because you'll feel less anxious about them. You worry less about the potential outcomes because you recognize them as unrealistic.

You're also less likely to rush the process. When you slow down, you can better understand and evaluate your options. You can carefully review pertinent information and insights related to them. You can apply reason, critical thinking, and intentionality to your choices.

So, let's talk about how you can apply a slower pace to your decision-making process.

Allow Yourself More Time

Emergencies aside, you generally have more time than you think to make decisions. Despite the pressure you feel, there's rarely a genuine need to decide at that moment. The urgency is often manufactured rather than legitimate.

There's risk attached to every nontrivial decision you make. Depending on your circumstances, your choices can jeopardize:

- Your finances
- Your relationships

- Your reputation
- Your career
- Your health
- Your safety
- Your legal status
- Your freedom
- Your leisure time

Slowing down mitigates the risk. It lets you thoroughly weigh your potential choices' pros and cons. You're less likely to overlook important details. Less likely to choose out of fear or external pressure. Less likely to make decisions you'll regret down the road.

So take your time. Think through your options. Analyze relevant data. Reflect on your values. Seek input from others. Consider the long-term effects of your choices. Review your options in the event your decisions lead to poor outcomes.

Allowing yourself more time doesn't guarantee you'll make good decisions. Nor will it eliminate the risk. However, it *will* alleviate many of the hazards that arise from rushing the decision-making process.

Eliminate Options

Having options is good. Having too *many* options is bad. It paralyzes you, sapping your confidence and imposing an undue burden on your cognitive resources. Imagine visiting the grocery store, intent on buying salad dressing, and facing dozens of exciting options. It's hard to choose from among them. This is known as choice overload or overchoice.

Choice overload typically slows down decision-making. But it can also cause you to rush the process. You start to feel overwhelmed and make hair-trigger decisions just to move forward. Just to overcome the indecision.

This is a recipe for future regret.

The best way to avoid this problem is to eliminate as many options as possible at the outset. Take the time to review them in light of your purpose. You'll find that many of them are extraneous or irrelevant.

For example, suppose again you're at the grocery store to buy a new salad dressing. Upon seeing the dozens of brands and flavors, you're about to make a knee-jerk decision in frustration. But let's say you want a *healthy* salad dressing. This means you can eliminate those that contain high fructose corn syrup. You can disregard 90% of your options. They undermine your purpose.

The next time you're tempted to rush a decision because you face too many options, slow down and review them based on what you want to achieve. Then, weed out the ones that detract from that goal.

Ask Probing Questions

Some of your decisions will be profoundly consequential. They'll involve big stakes and considerable risks, and choosing poorly can have costly repercussions. Here, it pays to slow down and ask yourself probing purposeful questions. These questions will encourage you to pause and reflect rather than make a hasty decision you'll regret later.

The next time you're at a crossroads and unsure what to do, ask yourself the following:

- What am I trying to accomplish?
- Does this decision support my values?
- What are the potential long-term consequences?
- What would cause me to regret this decision?
- Must I make this decision right now?
- Do I have enough information?
- What happens if I do nothing?
- What am I giving up as a result of this decision?
- I'm solely responsible for this decision. How do I feel about that?
- How will I know if I've made the right decision?

Reflecting on these questions forces you to slow down and consider the complexities that accompany important decisions. It gives you a chance to see your options in a variety of valuable contexts. Rather than boiling down the decision-making process to a simplistic action-oriented formula, it encourages you to ask what matters most to you and why.

In short, it gives you clarity.

Embrace "I Don't Know"

People look favorably on those who radiate confidence. One of the ways this confidence manifests is in making fast decisions. We appear competent and certain of our abilities when we make snap decisions. We seem bold, assertive, and determined.

Others respond by holding us in high regard. They ask us for advice. They look to us for leadership. They see us as experts, treating our opinions as facts. It's easy to get caught up in others' admiration and fall into the habit of seeking their praise.

The irony is that snap decisions often indicate impulsivity and recklessness. Rather than springing from our competency and confidence, they're prompted by our emotions. The praise and validation we receive are intoxicating, and we begin to believe the hype about ourselves. So, we continue to make on-the-spot decisions if only to maintain the facade.

The quickest way to curb this tendency is to say, "I don't know." To admit uncertainty. To recognize that you may lack the details you need to make a wise and informed choice. When you say, "I don't know," you acknowledge the complexity and potential impact of the decision you're facing and permit yourself to approach it thoughtfully.

These three simple words are powerful. They're honest. They're authentic. They also interrupt the tendency to seek others' validation by making spontaneous decisions.

Paradoxically, you gain credibility when you admit you

don't know how to proceed. Rather than arousing doubt, others begin to feel they can trust you. Your vulnerability resonates with them. They can relate to it.

When you slow down your decision-making process, you make better, smarter, more informed choices. You give yourself more time to think critically, review data, and mull over contingencies. You have more time to make sure your decisions align with your goals and values. You have time to view your options from multiple perspectives.

In this light, the benefits of rushing your decisions are trivial compared to the advantages of taking your time.

YOUR ROUTINES

> We are what we repeatedly do. Excellence, then, is not an act, but a habit.

> — ARISTOTLE

We enjoy the idea of being spontaneous. We like to think of ourselves as free-spirited, open-minded, and able to respond well to dynamic circumstances. These traits suggest a playful adaptability and enthusiasm for life.

The reality is that we thrive on structure. Most of us enjoy having routines that guide us regarding what to do and when. Our routines give us a sense of control because they make our daily lives more predictable. They lower our stress by alleviating our need to think about every repetitive task. We do them on autopilot.

For example, think about what you do after waking up each morning. You make your bed, use the restroom, brush your teeth, shower, shave or apply makeup, get dressed, gulp down a cup of coffee, and dash out the door. You don't have to think about these activities because they're a part of your morning routine. You're on autopilot.

The problem is that many of our routines are rushed. We move through them as quickly as possible. Instead of using them to feel calm and lower our stress, we use them to speed through our lives. Instead of giving us a sense of control, they reinforce our frantic, always-on-the-go lifestyle.

But as with every other area of your life, you can slow down your routines. Rather than speeding through them, you can take your time. When you do so, you get to savor moments that are usually sacrificed to support the busyness of your day.

Slow Down Your Mornings

Your morning routine should be calming. It should help you ease into your day rather than scrambling, anxious about what's on the horizon. It should also allow you to reflect on the things you value and recommit to being mindful of them as your day evolves.

But it's easy to get into the habit of rushing through your morning routine. Rather than calming, it becomes a daily struggle to cross off items as quickly as possible. To mark tasks as done rather than enjoy the experience of doing them.

Your mornings set the tone for the rest of your day. If you want to adopt a slower-paced lifestyle, you must commit to giving yourself time to start your day on the right foot. Here are three quick suggestions to help you overcome the urge to rush your early-day routine:

1. **Set aside a comfortable time chunk**. Give yourself enough time to go through your routine at a leisurely pace. You'll be less inclined to treat it as a set of tasks on a to-do list.

2. **Remember why you're following a morning routine**: mental clarity, reduced stress, improved focus, time to reflect, more intentionality, etc. Routines put your brain on autopilot. This tip helps you step back and reengage.

3. **Wake up earlier**. Giving yourself time is impossible if you lack the time you need. Waking up earlier solves this problem. Take baby steps. Wake up 10 minutes earlier each morning for one week. Then, wake up 10 minutes earlier each morning the following week. Continue doing this until you can complete your morning routine at a relaxed pace.

These three simple tips will help you resist the temptation to rush through your mornings. They'll encourage you to take your time, engage, and fully immerse yourself in them.

Slow Down Your Evenings

You have a morning routine that relaxes you, clears your head, and puts you in a good mood. But what about your evenings? What do you do after spending the day working at your job, handling your commitments, managing your responsibilities, and putting out fires?

You're worn out but still wound up. You're tired but wired. Your mind won't let go of the day's events, making it difficult to get to sleep despite being exhausted. You may even compound the issue by trying to get more done before bed.

This is an act of self-sabotage. By rushing around in the evening, you maintain high cortisol levels. Cortisol is the body's primary stress hormone, and one of its effects is to keep you awake. That's fine in the morning and afternoon. But it'll rob you of quality sleep in the evening. You'll wake up feeling unrested and fatigued, setting the stage for brain fog, high stress, and irritability throughout the day.

With that in mind, here are three things you can do to adopt a slower, more relaxing evening routine:

1. **Indulge in leisure reading**. It'll calm your mind, ease stress, and even bring down your heart rate. If you do it each night, your mind will gradually get the hint that it's nearly time for bed. You'll get to sleep faster and likely sleep better. Now's the time to read that engaging novel you set aside a while back. It's not the time to read the latest study related to your profession.

2. **Journal about your day**. Reflect on the positive things that happened. Let go of the negative things. And don't worry about your spelling or grammar. This is for your eyes only. No one will see it unless you want them to.

3. **Implement a no-device policy 60 minutes before bedtime**. It's tempting to send one last email from your laptop while in bed. It's hard to resist checking your phone for last-minute texts from family, friends, and coworkers. But these gadgets emit blue light, which suppresses melatonin, the body's sleep hormone. Additionally, texts and emails *stimulate* the brain rather than relax it.

There are many other things you can do to slow down your evenings. But start with these three. They'll relax your mind and body. They'll help you to wind down and prepare for sleep. Keep in mind that you can always experiment with other calming evening activities down the road.

Introduce Mindful Daytime Routines

Your morning and evening routines will help you to adopt a slower pace. But they're not enough. The time between them can still sabotage you if you allow it.

It's easy to get caught up in — and overwhelmed by — the day's chaos despite starting your morning on the right foot. You get distracted by others' demands for your attention. You find yourself putting out fires, robbed of the time and energy you need to address your responsibilities. Your priorities and needs get sidelined as your colleagues, bosses, and clients pull you in other directions.

You're exhausted when the day finally ends. Your evening routine relaxes you, but it won't save you. After all, the chaos will likely repeat itself tomorrow and sweep you up in its wake.

Unless you plan a few calming daytime routines.

You (hopefully) take breaks throughout your day. But what do you do on your breaks? Do you immediately check your phone for texts? Do you aimlessly scroll through social media? Do you rush around, trying to get non-work-related items done in the minutes you have available?

I recommend taking a more mindful approach. One that allows you to step away from the chaos and recharge. Here are a few calming activities you can do during a 10-minute break to lower your stress and restore your energy and balance.

- **Take a short walk**. Go outside. Enjoy the fresh air. Get some sunlight.
- **Practice deep breathing**. Inhale deeply and exhale fully ten times. You can do this while taking a walk.
- **Do stretching exercises**. Stretch your quads, calves, hamstrings, shoulders, triceps, and neck.
- **Journal**. Express gratitude, write about your aspirations, or reflect on the last few hours.
- **Play with your pet**. Play fetch or hide-and-seek. Do food puzzles. Do training games. Or just cuddle with them.

String together these and other relaxing activities, and you'll have a simple daytime routine you can lean on whenever you feel overwhelmed.

The takeaway is that you have more control over the pace of your day than you might imagine. Much of it depends on your routines. If you practice mindful morning, evening, and daytime routines that allow you to detach from the day's mayhem, you'll be less likely to get pulled into its current.

FINAL THOUGHTS ON THE ART OF GOING SLOW

~

We put our happiness on hold when we lead hectic, chaotic lives. We might *think* we're happy as we rush from one thing to another. We might try to convince ourselves that the hustle-and-grind lifestyle fulfills us. We might believe we're content as we're swept up by the whirlwind of other people's demands and priorities.

But we're not.

We want to relax. We want to reflect, learn, and grow. We want to connect with our loved ones and share meaningful experiences with them rather than merely log time. We want to pursue our hobbies and interests at our own leisurely pace.

But it's so easy to put our needs and priorities on the back burner as we try to keep up with today's hyper-paced world. We postpone our contentment and defer our aspirations to adapt to the fast rhythm of life's treadmill.

For example, have you ever promised yourself that you'll get around to a particular project or goal when things finally slow down?

- "I'm going to write that novel."
- "I'm going to travel."
- "I'm going to take my family on a vacation."
- "I'm going to get into shape."
- "I'm going to volunteer."
- "I'm going to finish my education."
- "I'm going to learn how to play the guitar."
- "I'm going to learn how to cook."
- "I'm going to start a ministry."

As time passes, these projects and goals remain in limbo. Due to neglect, they eventually wither on the vine.

But there's good news! You can *choose* to slow down. You can decide to adopt a slower-paced, less-hurried lifestyle. You can resolve today to step off life's treadmill and turn your back on hustle culture. When you do so, you'll give yourself the time, energy, freedom, and permission to focus on things that matter *to you*.

It won't be easy. It'll be like slowing a freight train if you've lived a hectic, urgent, fast-paced life for a while. There's a lot of momentum to counter.

The steps you've learned in this book will help you to overcome it. To reverse it. You now possess every tool you need to change gears and ease into the slow lane. To adopt a more relaxed pace. To embrace a slower, more mindful, intentional, and gratifying rhythm.

Take it one step at a time. Allow yourself to make mistakes. Reflect on them, learn from them, and let them go.

Acknowledge your small wins along the way. I assure you there will be many of them. Celebrate them. Take joy in them, knowing that each one brings you closer to the rewarding, enriching, and exhilarating life you desire.

MAY I ASK YOU A SMALL FAVOR?

~

Thanks so much for reading *The Art Of Going SLOW*. I know you're busy, and I greatly appreciate your choosing to spend time with me.

If you enjoyed reading *The Art Of Going SLOW*, please leave a short review on Amazon. A sentence or two about something you liked would mean the world to me, and your words will encourage others to read the book.

One last thing before we part ways (for now). I plan to write a few more books over the next twelve months. I'll likely release each of them at a steep discount for a limited time; you'll be able to grab each one for less than $1.

If you'd like to be notified when these books are released and take advantage of the discounted price, join my mailing list. When you do, you'll receive my 40-page

PDF ebook titled *Catapult Your Productivity! The Top 10 Habits You Must Develop to Get More Things Done.* You can join my list here:

http://artofproductivity.com/free-gift/

I'll also send you my best productivity and time management tips via my email newsletter. You'll receive tactics and strategies for beating procrastination, creating healthy morning routines, avoiding burnout, and developing razor-sharp focus, along with many other productivity hacks!

If you have questions or would like to share a tip, technique, or mind hack that has made a positive difference in your life, please feel free to reach out to me at damon@artofproductivity.com. I'd love to hear from you!

Until next time,

Damon Zahariades
http://artofproductivity.com

ABOUT THE AUTHOR

Damon Zahariades is a corporate refugee who endured years of unnecessary meetings, drive-by chats with coworkers, and a distraction-laden work environment before striking out on his own. Today, in addition to writing a growing catalog of time management and productivity books, he's the showrunner for the productivity blog Artof-Productivity.com.

In his spare time, he enjoys playing chess, poker, and the occasional video game with friends. And he continues to promise himself that he'll start playing the guitar again.

Damon lives in Southern California with his beautiful, supportive wife and their affectionate, quirky, and sometimes mischievous dog. He's looking wistfully at his 50th birthday in the rearview mirror.

OTHER BOOKS BY DAMON ZAHARIADES

∼

THINK BIG

How to Lead a Disciplined Life

The Mental Toughness Handbook

The Procrastination Cure

To-Do List Formula

80/20 Your Life!

The Time Chunking Method

How to Make Better Decisions

The Art of Living Well series

The Art Of Saying NO

The Art of Letting GO

The Art of Finding FLOW

The 30-Day Productivity Boost series

The 30-Day Productivity Plan - VOLUME I

The 30-Day Productivity Plan - VOLUME II

Self-Help Books for Busy People series

Small Habits Revolution

The Joy Of Imperfection

The P.R.I.M.E.R. Goal Setting Method

Improve Your Focus and Mental Discipline series

Fast Focus

Morning Makeover

Digital Detox

Visit ArtofProductivity.com for a complete list of titles and summaries. All titles are available for purchase in ebook, paperback, hardcover, and audiobook formats at ArtofProductivity.com/Amazon.

Made in the USA
Las Vegas, NV
23 March 2025

19988701R00105